CAREER POWER!

CAREER POWER!

A Manual for Personal Career Advancement

RICHARD J. RINELLA

CLAIRE C. ROBBINS

A DIVISION OF AMERICAN MANAGEMENT ASSOCIATIONS

Library of Congress Cataloging in Publication Data

Rinella, Richard J.
    Career power!

    1.Job hunting.   2.Vocational guidance.
    3.Resumes (Employment)   4.Employment interviewing.
I.   Robbins, Claire C., joint author.   II.   Title.
HF5382.7.R56 1981   650.1'4   80-69683
ISBN 0-8144-5630-8
ISBN 0-8144-7586-8 pbk

First AMACOM paperback edition 1982.

ACKNOWLEDGMENTS

We are most indebted to our clients who, over the years of our professional work, helped us to formulate the concepts and ideas that gave birth to this book.

Our special thanks to Catharine Conheim, who offered us a different perspective.

Everett Hano and Leanora Stephanoff gave us much insight and courage to pursue this journey. Thanks to Kathy Seigel for her "knowing"; to Linda Lee and Adrianne Battin for their example; to Sydney Amos for her unfailing support in editing and typing and bringing a sense of humor to us; to Mel Thompson, Eli Djeddah, and Bill Morin for believing in our work; and to Rob Kaplan, an editor extraordinaire.

A very special acknowledgment to Mr. "Z," who led us gently to insight and never allowed us to stray from the path.

Richard J. Rinella
Claire C. Robbins

CONTENTS

INTRODUCTION

You are embarking on a journey of vivid importance and telling consequence. This particular journey is called a career. Whether you are at the start of this adventure, or at a fork in the road, or about to reembark after a stopping point along the way, there are important things for you to know in order to successfully complete the trip. Let's look for a moment at the needs of any excursion. What do you need to know? What soundings do you need to take? What are the questions to ask that will serve you best?

- Where are you?
- What have you brought with you so far?
- Where are you going?
- What will be useful for you to take along?
- How can you get there?
- Who, if anyone, will accompany or aid you on this trip?
- What will help make your journey more efficient and pleasurable?

Your primary task is to answer these questions and see your way clear to making the most effective use of all this material in your career advancement. This manual is designed to help you do that. As you begin to define or redefine your career power and to envision your own career destination, you will develop a growing sense of security and assurance that the results will soon lead to a new and rewarding position.

This manual is your training coach. It will elicit from you pertinent data to lighten your task. It will ask you to participate in exercises that will reveal your total resources and help you focus on what you have done, can do, and will do. It will provide you with sample materials to serve as models. It will remind you of your goal and provide you with a medium to assess where you are and what your next step should be.

A natural momentum will develop as you follow this process. Past experience has shown that those individuals who work diligently at their preparation and search efforts will be successful. Reward comes through a disciplined, systematic series of actions.

We urge you not to jump into job interviews until you are ready. It is usually better to stay away from your primary targets until you have gotten your act together. You do not want to jeopardize your chances of landing the job you really want.

You will soon discover that you have been presented with a rare opportunity—to take stock of yourself and your future; to broaden your thinking and vision; to go where you want to go, do what you want to do. Your efforts will make this one of the more unusual and stimulating experiences of your life.

A positive attitude is essential to success. You have acquired skills and experience over the years, and there is a position out there waiting for someone like you. All you have to do is find it. This manual will show you how.

You have, at hand, an exciting and challenging job: namely, to research, package, and market yourself. You can approach this assignment with the same vigor, imagination, and discipline that you would approach any other, even if this particular perspective is new to you.

Do not expect to see success overnight. Be patient. You will reach your goal.

To Those Entering the Job Market

You, too, have marketable skills and experience. There is no way you could have reached your present age without developing them. You may not now see what they are; it will be your task to delve into your personal history and reveal the resources that are there.

To Those Making a Career Switch

Part of the task before you is an opportunity to translate what you have already accomplished in one career area to another area in such a way that you can present a potent picture of yourself to employers in the new field. You need not throw away anything you've learned and developed; you will see how to utilize past experience to lead you to an image of the new experience you want for yourself.

To Those Seeking Career Advancement

You will need to take a sounding of your present strengths and assets and match them with those most valued in your chosen field. You will also benefit by seeing how to develop those qualities to their fullest and to place maximum weight on them. To be stuck indicates that either you don't know how, or think you don't know how, to make progress—or that some obstacle is in your way.

Many people today feel that their job is boring, stressful, and unrewarding. It is common to see people changing jobs. Look around you at the number of people who are underemployed, underpaid, or misemployed.

A more dramatic way to respond to the stress of an unrewarding job is to venture into an entirely new career. In a national survey conducted in 1976, the Bureau of Labor Statistics reported that approximately 5.5 million Americans were working in an occupation different from the one they were engaged in one year earlier.

Just what is happening?

Many of us start our working life with little knowledge of the demands and pressures we may face. We have insufficient knowledge about ourselves—our strengths, weaknesses, and job preferences. As we grow and mature, we discover that our needs, interests, and expectations about life and work change. This is a normal part of our makeup as people. And these changing needs and expectations lead to changes of desired work style and work orientation.

You may know men and women who are readying themselves for jobs and job changes by preparing resumes, calling friends for leads, and answering want ads. Perhaps you even know some who are readying themselves for career changes by enrolling in college and extension courses to retool a skill or to learn a new vocation, in the hopes of finding career satisfaction in a new field. All of this may be in perspective, but to pursue these efforts without an understanding of the realities of who you are and what the job market is, is to run the risk of being pushed or dropped into jobs that misemploy or underuse your abilities and interests and lead nowhere.

This band-aid answer to job frustration is frequently a route to further frustration. You are to be congratulated for choosing a different route.

Through the Career Power guidance process discussed in this manual, you will learn how to see yourself realistically—as a productive human being entering, relocating, or advancing in the commercial and professional world. *Career Power!* is structured to assist you to do some vital short- and long-range career planning, assess those things in your life and work that are gratifying, identify problem-solving skills that can be channeled to your work, and adopt work objectives that are in harmony with your expectations. This discovery or rediscovery will take energy and effort. If you are willing to roll up your sleeves and work with the process, you will have a sure handle on selecting a realistically rewarding career and mapping out your personal plan to realize job satisfaction.

The program presented in this manual is also highly structured to help you become your own best job search agent. It will provide you with the tools to identify your job accomplishments, prepare results-oriented resumes, write attention-getting letters, manage a successful job search, and develop essential interviewing techniques. With this knowledge base, you will be successful in getting what you want.

In addition, you will be introduced to methods of ongoing evaluation, to enable you to assess your new job, as well as yourself and your relationships on the job, so that you can anticipate and head off difficulties and frustrations. With these skills, you will be successful in maintaining and enhancing what you get.

The next section will give you a more detailed overview of the contents of the manual. This will help you grasp more specifically the work you will be doing.

OVERVIEW

Section 1   Identifying Your Job Skills

You will begin the work by tuning in to the many perspectives of your personal resources and attitudes that will enable you to make meaningful and realistic career choices. You will learn to develop, for yourself and for future employers, a fuller picture of your real accomplishments. You will begin to establish a match between yourself and a future position.

Section 2   Packaging Your Skills
In this segment of the work, you will develop a resume, one of the tools of an effective marketing strategy.

Section 3   Advertising Your Skills
In this portion of the work, you will research the job marketplace to ensure that what you want is obtainable. You will develop an individualized plan to market yourself. And you will initiate a variety of steps to either find or generate the job you want.

Section 4   Selling Your Skills and Signing the Contract
This part of the work will prepare you, in a variety of ways, to be a confident and skilled interviewee. You will learn how to make the most of an interview session and how to present yourself in the most favorable light. You will prepare yourself to respond to job offers with tact and good judgment and to negotiate the salary and conditions you want.

Section 5   Planning Your Strategies for Upward Mobility
Now that you've achieved your short-term goal, you will train yourself to build and maintain healthy conditions on the job—within yourself, with others, and within your role. You will learn to establish an ongoing evaluation to ensure that you stay in this position as long as, and no longer than, it is in your best interests to do so.

Appendixes
We will help you define management functions and provide a reference list to aid you in researching the marketplace.

Section 1

IDENTIFYING
YOUR JOB SKILLS

The work in this section is all based on a premise that can be expressed in the formula: self-awareness + skill utilization = realized career potential. We have no doubt that you want to realize your career potential. These exercises will enable you to reach a level of meaningful self-understanding and to examine pertinent areas of your personal makeup and life-style that contribute to achieving this fulfillment in your life. To accomplish this, you will need to see clearly and to tune in distinctly to your most valuable assset: yourself. It is important to look at yourself with no interference from a fogged-up filter and to tune into yourself without the distortion of static. In other words, to know yourself afresh, to perceive anew.

So, as you answer all the questions that are put to you, whether or not you see their immediate relevance, you will be mirroring the real you. You will be stretching your mind and your horizons. The energy you put into this work will have a powerful payoff.

NEGATIVE RAP SESSION

Everyone has a job. Whether you are a military officer, an advertising executive, a secretary, a teacher, a housewife, a leader in the PTA, a plumber, a student working part time, an engineer, a salesperson—you've been spending your time and energy at a job! For now, we want you to focus on your negative associations to this position—your resentments, dissatisfactions, and other gripes. Although this kind of activity may not be part of your usual style, and you may not now see the positive purpose in it, you will be led through this negativity to a sound and advantageous conclusion. So allow yourself to enter this task with energy and thoroughness. Don't try to be "fair." Don't try to see the "other side." For now, let yourself spill out these negative feelings, whether they are about the work itself; about the quantity of the work; about the work environment; about your colleagues, your boss, your subordinates; about your unrealized expectations of the job; about the way the job continues or has ended. Use the page provided to write down all of your gripes. Whatever you come up with that's real for you is right for this exercise. You may repeat what you've already told colleagues, or say for the first time what you've never dared to express out loud, or even allow yourself to see what before now you had kept hidden, even from yourself. Don't get sidetracked by spelling, grammar, language. Just let it flow, watch it come out. Take all the time you need, and all the space.

MY GRIPES

MORE GRIPES

_____

_____

_____

_____

_____

_____

_____

_____

_____

_____

_____

_____

_____

TURNING GRIPES INTO "WOWS"

As you worked at that exercise, the odds are that you experienced a range of emotions—anger, sadness, righteousness, satisfaction, amusement being just a few of them. If you didn't hold back, you should now feel a sense of release from addressing the negatives of this past, perhaps ongoing, experience. You've been letting off steam! Now, steam is a source of energy that can be put to productive use, that can run machines, that can move and change what is. It's time to use this "steam" that you've just seen pouring out.

In this follow-up endeavor, take the core of what you've said and let yourself learn a "wow!" from it:

"Wow, from this I can learn _____ ."
"Wow, from this I can understand _____ ."
"Wow, from this I can get a handle on _____ ."
"Wow, from this I can tell myself that _____ ."

No doubt, a few examples will help you to understand more easily how you can squeeze meaning and good for yourself from the complaints you expressed.

"He was always there, looking over my shoulder. I could hardly breathe without my supervisor (spouse, partner) wanting to know what I was doing, when I would be finished, what I had accomplished so far. Wow, from this I can see that I need space in my next position to complete a task at my own speed and to evaluate it for myself before anyone else takes a look at what I've been doing."

"Nobody trained me. Nobody told me anything about how to do my job. I had to put the whole thing together myself. Well, I did it, of course; I always come through. But my family began to think I was insufferable. After a day at the office, I could hardly stomach them either. And of course, now my blood pressure is up. Not really high, mind you, but up. Wow, from this it's very obvious that, although I can handle a one-person operation in terms of responsibility, my health and well-being will suffer when I don't have a collaborative atmosphere to work in. I can tell from this experience that I need, for myself and my family, to ask for assistance and for instruction and not to shoulder it all alone."

"Well, I was there at 8:00 and I left at 6:00. And I did what was expected of me. And more. I did a good job, got along with everybody, received good quarterly ratings. I don't have any complaints about the work; it's just that I never got to be in on the finish of any of the projects. I planned, designed, developed the prototypes—as ordered. Good job. And then someone else took it from there. And where was I? I couldn't find any meaning in my work. Wow, from this I can hear a loud message that I want and need a job where I'm part of a project from beginning to end. I want to be able to look at a product and really feel connected to it. That'll give meaning to all those hours I spend at the office."

"It's hard to say what I'm mad about, except that I was always a little embarrassed to tell people what I did. It's not that there's anything wrong with being an office manager. I like the responsibility, the diversity of tasks. I'm good at delegating, at overseeing others at their jobs. I can anticipate difficulties, and I'm great at problem solving. I don't even mind the routine. But somehow I can't really get behind pesticides. I know they're needed in agriculture and elsewhere, but I was embarrassed to be a part of it. Wow, from this I'm learning that not only is it important to me what functions I perform in my work, but the nature and output of the company I work for are really vital in terms of whether I can put my all into my job."

Perhaps these examples not only have given you an idea of how to start finding the "wows" in your own complaints but have triggered additional complaints. If this is true for you, go back to your list of gripes and write down whatever new irritants you got in touch with. Then, turn to the next page and start uncovering your "wows." There is no right or wrong to this work. What you discover here will be the beginning of an evaluation tool, designed expressly by you, that you will be able to apply to any future job you consider. What you come up with here, we will be using again and again as a compass for finding your best direction.

MY "WOWS"

POTENTIAL CAREER CHOICES

You will now undertake an assignment in "hunching." Knowing yourself as you do at the moment, ask yourself which career directions you "hunch" may be suited to your skills.

To aid you in this process, we have prepared three comprehensive lists. The first names 25 major industries. Begin your "hunching" exercise by reviewing this list to determine which, if any, of these industries appeal to you. The second lists examples of career areas that are common to the 25 major industries. The third comprises examples of job classifications that are common within career areas.

Study these lists and then select those industries, careers, and jobs that you "hunch" may be potentials for you to pursue and jot them down in the space provided. As you move through the exercises to help you focus on your new job, you'll be asked to check back on the choices you made, to validate your decision.

Obviously, we have not listed all the types of jobs that are available, so if after searching this list you need further help, take some time out and study the titles published by the U.S. Department of Labor, Employment and Training Administration, available at your local college or public library.

MAJOR INDUSTRIES

Advertising	Engineering	Merchandising
Aerospace/High Technology	Entertainment/ Recreation	Nonprofit Organizations
Agriculture	Finance	Physical/Life Sciences
Architecture	Government	Real Estate
Art	Health	Religion
Communications	Hospitality	Social Sciences
Conservation	Insurance	Transportation
Construction	Law	
Consulting	Manufacturing	

EXAMPLES OF CAREER AREAS WITHIN INDUSTRIES

Advertising
  Public Relations
  Graphic Arts
  Writing
  Community Rela-
    tions

Aerospace/High Tech-
    nology
  Aircraft Manufactur-
    ing/Sales
  Computer Manufac-
    turing/Sales
  Aerospace Manufac-
    turing
  Energy/Environ-
    mental

Agriculture
  Forestry
  Farming
  Food Processing
  Crop/Food Inspec-
    tion

Architecture
  Design
  Landscaping
  Space Utilization

Art
  Photography
  Fashion
  Furniture
  Commercial
  Interior Design

Communications
  Data Processing
  Media (TV, radio)
  Publishing
  Technical Writing

Conservation
  Forestry
  Associations
  Energy

Construction
  Finance
  Administration
  Property Manage-
    ment
  Technical Engi-
    neering
  Facilities Layout
    and Design

Consulting
  Private Sector
  Public Sector
  Business Systems
  Personnel
  Management Devel-
    opment
  Technical
  Sales/Marketing
  International
  In-House Corporate

Engineering
  Technical
  Facilities/Plant En-
    gineering
  Packaging
  Industrial
  Administrative Sup-
    port
  Sales

Entertainment/Recre-
    ation
  Athletics
  Leisure
  Media

Production
  Acting

Finance
  Accounting
  Investments
  Budgets
  Research
  Banking
  Estate Planning
  Credit/Collections
  Endowments
  Bookkeeping
  Government Finan-
    cial Aid

Government
  Social Work
  City Management
  County Administra-
    tion
  Transportation
  Urban Planning
  Police/Fire Protec-
    tion
  Financial Adminis-
    tration
  Health/Hospitals
  Employment Ser-
    vices

Health
  Nursing
  Counseling
  Dentistry
  Veterinary Science
  Physical Therapy
  Pharmaceuticals
  Cosmetology
  Funeral Direction
  Chiropractics

Nutrition
Rehabilitation
Safety
General Medicine

Hospitality
Hotel
Motel
Conventions

Insurance
Life
Casualty
Underwriting
Actuary
Administration

Law
Paralegal
Administration/Office Management
Research
Enforcement
Contracts
Court Administration
Corporate Law

Manufacturing
Production
Scheduling

Fabrication
Purchasing
Financial
Legal
Marketing
Sales
Administration

Merchandising
Retail
Wholesale
Procurement/Buying
Administration

Nonprofit Organizations
United Way Agencies
Associations
Foundations
Hospital Volunteer Services

Physical/Life Sciences
Chemistry
Physics
Botany
Zoology
Physical Education

Real Estate

Escrow
Residential Sales
Commercial/Industrial Sales
Appraisal
Property Management
Investments

Religion
Fund Raising
Clerical
Administration

Social Sciences
Social Welfare
Psychology
Politics
Sociology
Human Resource Development
Education
Home Economics
History

Transportation
Traffic
Shipping
Sales
Marketing

EXAMPLES OF JOB CLASSIFICATIONS WITHIN CAREER AREAS

Endowments/Foundations
  Grant Writer—Nonprofit Ventures
  Fund Raiser
  General Administrator
  Publicity Writer

Bookkeeping
  Accounts Receivable Clerk
  Accounts Payable Clerk
  Billing Clerk
  Payroll Clerk

Hotel/Motel
  Salesperson
  Administrator
  Caterer
  Reservations Clerk
  Food/Beverage Buyer

Conventions
  Salesperson
  Administrator
  Facilities Coordinator
  Engineer

Social Welfare
  Social Worker—Civil Service
  Social Worker—Private Agency
  Alcoholic/Drug Counselor
  Fund Raiser

Psychology
  Psychiatric Social Worker
  Testing/Measurement Technician
  Psychological Aide
  Teacher

Investments
  Stocks/Bonds Salesperson
  Real Estate Salesperson
  Corporate Business Planner
  Mutual Funds Salesperson

Wholesale Stock Trader

Budgets
  Budget Administrator—Corporate
  Personal/Family Budget Planner
  Accountant

Financial Research
  Stock/Bond Researcher
  Financial Analyst
  Paralegal
  Pollster
  Marketing/Sales Analyst

Purchasing
  Buyer (clothing, machines, food, production, parts)
  Retail Department Store Buyer
  Importer/Exporter
  Pricing Analyst

Data Processing
  Programmer
  Key-Punch Operator
  Mathematician
  Work Scheduler
  Administrator
  Systems Analyst

Personnel/Employee Relations
  Labor Relations Analyst
  Wage and Salary Specialist
  Employment Interviewer
  Employee Benefits Specialist
  Management Development and Training Specialist
  Job Classifications Analyst

Administrative Services
  House Organ Writer
  Management Systems Analyst
  Community Relations Coordinator

Recreation Employee Services
   Administrator
Budget Specialist

Education
   Program Development Researcher
   Fund Raiser
   Career Counselor
   Teacher
   Facilities/Maintenance Specialist
   Transportation Driver
   Office Administrator

Marketing
   Researcher
   Copywriter
   Customer Service Representative
   Pricing Analyst
   Contracts Administrator
   Public/Community Relations
      Specialist

Sales
   Customer Service Representative
   Telephone Solicitor

After-Sales Service Specialist
Contract Administrator
Salesperson (services/products)

Accounting
   Budget Analyst
   Accounts Receivable Clerk
   Accounts Payable Clerk
   Billing Administrator
   Bookkeeper
   Cost/Price Analyst
   Long-Range Business Planning
      Specialist
   Statistician

Production
   Machine Design and Layout
      Engineer
   Scheduler
   Parts and Supplies Coordinator
   Fabrication Specialist
   Facilities Layout Engineer
   Industrial Engineer
   Budget Analyst

MY "HUNCHES"

Industries

1. _____

2. _____

3. _____

Career Areas

1. _____

2. _____

3. _____

4. _____

5. _____

6. _____

Jobs

1. _____
2. _____
3. _____
4. _____
5. _____
6. _____
7. _____
8. _____

FEELING GOOD ABOUT YOUR WORK

The groups of questions in this section have been designed to elicit data about your likes, dislikes, strengths, and interests so that you will be able to make a happier match between yourself and your future job.

Give yourself time in answering these self-exploratory questions to picture the "you" you're speaking about, to get a grasp on your multifaceted nature. Give yourself the gift of straightforwardness, and don't be afraid to take some risks.

A. Think about how you choose to spend your time outside of work or would choose to spend additional time if you had it. Then, list some of the activities that give you satisfaction and add those aspects of the very same activities that limit your enjoyment or satisfaction.

Examples:

> "I like to make furniture (but I don't like having to do the final finish of the pieces with varnish or shellac or paint)."
> "I like to cook (but I don't like anyone else helping me chop the vegetables or do the seasoning)."
> "I like to coach kids sports (but I don't like it when some of the parents interfere with my decisions)."
> "I like to visit and chat with my friends and neighbors (but I don't like them just dropping in on me)."

List as many activities (along with the "buts") as you can think of:

I like to _____

(but I _____).

I like to _____

(but I _____).

I like to _____

(but I _____).

I like to _____

(but I _____).

I like to _____

(but I _____).

I like to _____

(but I _____).

B. Repeat the preceding exercise with examples from your work life. Examples:

"I like research (but I don't like writing up the reports)."

"I like meeting customers (but not for the very first time)."

"I like to analyze problems (but I get bored when the same problems keep surfacing)."

O.K., go to it.

I like to _____

(but I _____).

I like to _____

(but I _____).

I like to _____

(but I _____).

I like to _____

(but I _____).

I like to _____

(but I _____).

I like to _____

(but I _____).

I like to _____

(but I _____).

C. In your present or previous position, which aspects of your job did you enjoy the most? Give as many examples as possible. Be specific.

_____

_____

_____

_____

_____

_____

D. Upon completion of your formal schooling, which subjects did you continue to study or read about?

_____   _____

_____   _____

_____   _____

_____   _____

_____   _____

E. What was the best job you ever had? What were the elements that made it the best job? There are no "shoulds" about what makes a particular job appealing. Enjoy discovering what has made this particular job enjoyable for you.

_____

_____

_____

_____

_____

_____

F. If you were creating the perfect job for yourself, what would be the five features most important to you (responsibilities, peculiarities, rewards, location, whatever)?

1. _____

2. _____

3. _____

4. _____

5. _____

G1. If you were working with a flexible time schedule, what would you do with your "off" time?

_____

_____

_____

_____

_____

G2. How do you spend the nonworking, nonchore time you now have? List just those activities that take up the bulk of your free time.

1. _____ (____%)

2. _____ (____%)

3. _____ (____%)

4. _____ (____%)

5. _____ (____%)

G3. What conclusions can you draw about yourself and your actual preferences for the use of time by comparing G1 and G2?

_____

_____

_____

_____

_____

_____

H. What are five qualities you really admire about yourself (e.g., honesty, cooperativeness, creativeness)?

1. _____

2. _____

3. _____

4. _____

5. _____

I. What are five talents or capabilities that you're proud of (e.g., making people comfortable, doing arithmetic in your head, good at convincing people)?

1. _____

2. _____

3. _____

4. _____

5. _____

J. It's time to put together what you have learned from answering these questions. You're developing a composite picture of the ways in which you shine and what you do that you find personally rewarding. Here's how to begin. Right now, give yourself a temporary new name. Choose a name that you do not usually identify with, and write it down: _____ . There is a reason for this directive. Most of us maintain sometimes hazy, sometimes solid images of ourselves: how we are, what we like, what we're good at. When new data come our way that might alter this image, we inadvertently overlook the new information or discount it or forget we said it. The best way to get an accurate picture of ourselves is to move back, far enough away to refocus, and then to tell our story from that distance. Taking a temporary new name will help establish that necessary distance.

Now, in the space provided (plus any extra space you need) tell _____'s story. Read through all you've written on the preceding pages. Let a picture form of this person you've read about. Tune in to the ways to speak of this person that will ring true. Now remove yourself slightly, move back a little. And begin.

"This is _____'s story. Let me tell you what I now know about him/her and about the kinds of situations and activities that I realize are meaningful and feel good to him/her. I want to summarize what I've learned so that you too can get a feeling for what _____ is like. First of all, _____

_____

_____

_____

_____

_____

_____

AND NOT FEELING SO GOOD

All of us participate in chores or responsibilities that we mildly or actively dislike—the kinds of activities that we would like to make vanish by snapping our fingers or by having someone else take care of them for us.

A. Take a moment and note some of these activities here; include activities from both your personal and work life.

1. _____   5. _____

2. _____   6. _____

3. _____   7. _____

4. _____   8. _____

B. Now examine these activities from the perspective of finding out what aspects are displeasing (boring, difficult, offensive, frustrating, etc.) to you. Then, list your discoveries below.

Examples:

"I find vacuuming the house frustrating because it is a repetitive job that is barely completed before it needs redoing."

"Attending staff meetings makes me uncomfortable because I may be called on for a presentation before my peers."

"I find doing my taxes unpleasant because I need to attend to so many varied details that could cost me money if I missed them."

In other words, you have here the opportunity to learn from some "negatives" in your life by defining the particular features of activities that you will want to keep to a minimum as you design your working environment. Take the time to dig deeply for the hidden messages.

1. _____
   _____

2. _____
   _____

3. _____
   _____

4. _____
   _____

5. _____
   _____

6. _____

_____

7. _____

_____

8. _____

_____

C. You are to be given a magic wand. You can change any five aspects of your present (or previous) job. What will you change, and to what?

1. _____ to _____

2. _____ to _____

3. _____ to _____

4. _____ to _____

5. _____ to _____

D. List five qualities or characteristics that you believe limit, or could limit, you from reaching your desired potential in your career. After each, include a phrase or two describing the kind of impact you suspect this trait has made (or might make) on your career growth.
Examples:

"Impulsive (may accept first job offered even though it's not quite right for me)."
"Laugh a lot (some people may think I don't take my work seriously enough)."

1. _____

_____

2. _____

_____

3. _____

_____

4. _____

_____

5. _____

_____

E. Which, if any, of the qualities listed above would you like to change? How would you like to change them? What do you think would be the result of such a change? Be specific.
Example:

"I wish I found it easier to be more tactful. If I were, my energy wouldn't so frequently be needed to soothe hurt feelings and I could get a lot more out of a work day."

_____

_____

_____

_____

_____

_____

_____

_____

_____

_____

F. Identify the one event, or situation, that has most significantly frustrated your career growth. What, specifically, has been the negative impact of this situation?

_____

_____

_____

_____

_____

_____

_____

_____

_____

G. If you have ever been terminated from a job, what do you think were the reasons? Separate out the *external factors* (e.g., funding cut back; merger eliminated many jobs), the *interpersonal factors* (e.g., boss was threatened by you; difficulty communicating with some of the staff), and the *personal factors* (e.g., occasionally late with reports; never knew what was expected of you; bored with the job).

External factors:

_____

_____

_____

_____

_____

Interpersonal factors:

_____

_____

_____

_____

_____

Personal factors:

_____

_____

_____

_____

_____

H. Summing up: As you reread exercises A–G in this section, what are the two main pieces of advice you would give to the "you" revealed here as you consider a specific job? What you choose to say is important. Consider carefully.

1. _____

_____

_____

_____

_____

_____

_____

2. _____

_____

_____

_____

_____

_____

_____

_____

_____

_____

_____

MORE ABOUT ME

A. The following is a list of common personality traits. Review the list and check those traits you believe are true of you as a professional person.

__ kind	__ rigid	__ lazy	__ shy
__ patient	__ critical	__ flexible	__ tense
__ articulate	__ predictable	__ achiever	__ passive
__ workaholic	__ cheerful	__ quick to anger	__ pushy
__ ambitious	__ frustrated	__ lack goals	__ persuasive
__ practical	__ goal directed	__ unhappy	__ hate detail
__ self-motivated	__ relaxed	__ loyal	__ stubborn
__ dissatisfied	__ impatient	__ nitpicker	__ nervous
__ naive	__ analytical	__ team player	__ careful
__ intelligent	__ confused	__ independent	__ intimidated
__ disorganized	__ have poor	__ bored	__ trusting
__ imaginative	concentration	__ complacent	__ slow
__ erratic	__ pessimistic	__ impulsive	__ forgetful
__ initiator	__ argumentative	__ self-righteous	__ careless
__ defensive	__ dependent	__ brash	__ responsible

__ congenial   __ self-aggrandizing   __ intense   __ intimidating

__ opportunistic   __ arrogant   __ diligent   __ sympathetic

__ versatile

B. Without returning to the previous page and your responses there, review this list and check those personality traits you think best reflect what others (colleagues, supervisors, subordinates) would say about you.

__ kind	__ rigid	__ lazy	__ shy
__ patient	__ critical	__ flexible	__ tense
__ articulate	__ predictable	__ achiever	__ passive
__ workaholic	__ cheerful	__ quick to anger	__ pushy
__ ambitious	__ frustrated	__ lack goals	__ persuasive
__ practical	__ goal directed	__ unhappy	__ hate detail
__ self-motivated	__ relaxed	__ loyal	__ stubborn
__ dissatisfied	__ impatient	__ nitpicker	__ nervous
__ naive	__ analytical	__ team player	__ careful
__ intelligent	__ confused	__ independent	__ intimidated
__ disorganized	__ have poor	__ bored	__ trusting
__ imaginative	concentration	__ complacent	__ slow
__ erratic	__ pessimistic	__ impulsive	__ forgetful
__ initiator	__ argumentative	__ self-righteous	__ careless
__ defensive	__ dependent	__ brash	__ responsible
__ congenial	__ self-aggrandizing	__ intense	__ intimidating
__ opportunistic	__ arrogant	__ diligent	__ sympathetic
__ versatile			

C. (Optional) Offer this to your present or a (recent) previous supervisor and request that he or she complete it honestly and forthrightly.

Please review this list and check those personality traits that you think best reflect me as a professional person. Your straightforward response to this exercise will provide me with valuable feedback and will be much appreciated.

Thank you, _____

__ kind	__ rigid	__ lazy	__ shy
__ patient	__ critical	__ flexible	__ tense
__ articulate	__ predictable	__ achiever	__ passive
__ workaholic	__ cheerful	__ quick to anger	__ pushy
__ ambitious	__ frustrated	__ lack goals	__ persuasive
__ practical	__ goal directed	__ unhappy	__ hate detail
__ self-motivated	__ relaxed	__ loyal	__ stubborn
__ dissatisfied	__ impatient	__ nitpicker	__ nervous ·
__ naive	__ analytical	__ team player	__ careful
__ intelligent	__ confused	__ independent	__ intimidated
__ disorganized	__ have poor	__ bored	__ trusting
__ imaginative	concentration	__ complacent	__ slow
__ erratic	__ pessimistic	__ impulsive	__ forgetful
__ initiator	__ argumentative	__ self-righteous	__ careless
__ defensive	__ dependent	__ brash	__ responsible
__ congenial	__ self-aggrandizing	__ intense	__ intimidating
__ opportunistic	__ arrogant	__ diligent	__ sympathetic
__ versatile			

REACHING SOME CONCRETE CONCLUSIONS

A. Now look over the lists in the "More about Me" exercise. Start by identify-ing the mismatches, those qualities that you see in yourself that others probably don't see or those you don't believe are true about you that others would call you on. If you're comfortable or even delighted with the mismatch, fine! But when you find a mismatch that you are uncomfortable with, or that you suspect is a possible detriment to your relations with others or to your career advance-ment, you can use this awareness to make useful changes.

This is an opportunity, again, to put something "negative" to work in your behalf. Suppose, for example, that you believe yourself to be a team player but indicated that you doubt whether fellow workers see you as such. Ask yourself this question: "What are the particular behaviors (what do I do, show, say) that might lead others *not* to experience me as a team player?" Or come at it from the opposite vantage point. Suppose that you checked "critical" as a trait others pick up in you, although you don't usually feel particularly judgmental toward your colleagues. Again ask yourself: "What are the particular behaviors (what do I do or say, how do I look) that might lead others to experience me as critical?"

Go through the lists, identifying those mismatches you are unhappy with. Keep asking yourself what you are doing that creates this impression. Write down your answers here:

1. _____
_____

2. _____
_____

3. _____
_____

4. _____
_____

5. _____
_____

6. _____
_____

B. Now go back through the lists, seeking out any matches that create for you a similar discomfort. Again ask yourself what you do (or don't do) that creates this impression. Take as much space and time as necessary to really isolate those behaviors that are not beneficial to your work relationships or advancement. You don't at this point have to decide to change your behavior. You can allow yourself to take a clear sounding of how others see you without any commitment, at the present time, to do something about it. Be sure to write down the specific behaviors that create these views of you. It's an important part of the process.

1. _____
_____

2. _____
_____

3. _____
_____

4. _____
   _____

5. _____
   _____

6. _____
   _____

C1. Now once again review the lists. Choose one trait that you didn't check in list A of the "More about Me" exercise and would like to have honestly been able to check, for example, "self-motivated." Then finish this sentence:

I could be self-motivated if only _____
_____ .

Choose another trait and deal with it the same way:

I could be _____ if only _____

And another:

I could be _____ if only _____
_____ .

And another:

I could be _____ if only _____
_____ .

C2. Now, for each of these qualities you would like to have, do the following exercise. Choose a time when you were self-motivated (or whatever the desired trait) and list what was going on in that situation that contributed to your being self-motivated. What were others doing? How did you feel about them? What did you tell yourself about your own role? What did you show yourself about the situation? Off what external stimulus did you exhibit this quality? What were others contributing to your ability to act this way? Etc.

1. _____
   _____
   _____
   _____

2. _____
_____
_____
_____

3. _____
_____
_____
_____
_____

4. _____
_____
_____
_____

D1. In the preceding set of exercises, you had an opportunity to learn a great deal about your behaviors that may or may not reflect who you really are. You were looking at what you think others see when they observe you. This exercise will provide you with some additional information along these lines.

What adjectives would your spouse, parents, or friends use to describe you? If you run into any difficulty coming up with these, by all means look back at the list of traits under "More about Me" to help trigger your memory. Come up with at least ten words or phrases that they might use. Do not deliberately slant them to be either complimentary or critical.

1. _____   6. _____
2. _____   7. _____
3. _____   8. _____
4. _____   9. _____
5. _____   10. _____

D2. Once again you have a matching job to do that will give you important insight toward making the best of your capabilities. Compare these adjectives and phrases with the lists you completed on the preceding pages, and identify the *positive* qualities that you show at home and in social situations that you do not project in your professional capacity.

1. _____
2. _____
3. _____

4. _____

5. _____

These are advantageous resources that are already an established part of your behavioral repertoire. How would using each of these qualities at work enhance your professional image? What would it mean in terms of behavior change to use each quality at work? Be specific.

1. _____
   _____

2. _____
   _____

3. _____
   _____

4. _____
   _____

5. _____
   _____

(There is another important way to look at all this. What are the positive qualities that you exhibit at work that you keep hidden in your home and social situations? Although we will not devote space for you to answer this question here, answering it will give you a valuable personal gift. We highly recommend that you do it.)

E1. Summarize the attitudes that you believe your present (or previous supervisor) holds (or held) toward your job performance. My supervisor thinks that I:

1. _____

2. _____

3. _____

4. _____

5. _____

6. _____

7. _____

8. _____

E2. Which attitudes would you like your supervisor to eliminate from his or her view of your work performance?

1. _____

2. _____

3. _____

E3. What specific behaviors could you initiate to begin to change your supervisor's mind? Before you begin, read this sample:

"I think my supervisor sees me as being methodical and careful, but not as being as fast as I could be. I think he believes I am really responsible in doing the job but that I procrastinate. I believe he sees me as systematic and organized. I wish he didn't think of me as a procrastinator or as not speedy enough, as not efficient. What could I do to change these opinions about me?"

"I could involve him in the design of the system I use; I could get more of his input."

"I could talk to him to communicate the importance that I place on thoroughness to eliminate errors and explain to him that I think that initial thoroughness saves time in the long run and is therefore really an efficient way to proceed."

"I could set up a schedule that would show him that my plans allow sufficient time for me to accomplish various activities."

Study this sample to get your own thoughts flowing. Review your responses to E1 and E2 and give examples of specific new behaviors that would favorably affect your supervisor's attitude toward your job performance.

_____

_____

_____

_____

_____

_____

_____

_____

_____

_____

E4. Would these behavioral changes have been helpful in other jobs you've held? Would they be helpful for other phases of your life? How?

_____

_____

_____

_____

_____

_____

_____

_____

As a result of doing these exercises, you may find that you have a lot more control over what your supervisors or colleagues think of your performance than you had imagined. Indeed, you have more control over what you do on the job than perhaps you had previously given yourself credit for.

GET AT YOUR PROBLEM-SOLVING SKILLS

You possess a multitude of problem-solving skills, and it will be useful for you to enumerate them. Before you can do this, however, it is necessary to make the phrase _problem-solving skills_ more meaningful to you.

Let's go beyond the negative connotations of the word _problem_ and think of problems as any needs to be filled and goals to be accomplished as well as obstacles to be overcome. The basic element in the idea of work—whether it is at a job, at home, or in community affairs—is that there are goals to be achieved—that is, problems to be resolved. Therefore, all the talents and capabilities that you can use to accomplish a stated purpose are problem-solving skills. To be good at repairing machinery can fill a need. To be good at designing machinery can fill a need. To be good at getting people to follow your directions can fill a need. To be good at working collaboratively with others can fill a need.

These "good ats" are thus all examples of problem-solving skills. Inherent in each and every one of your personality strengths is at least one problem-solving skill. You said you were patient? Then chances are you are good at returning again and again to an unfinished task until it's completed. You said you were imaginative? Then chances are that you're good at generating creative ideas. Do you get the idea?

It is your problem-solving skills that enable your world to turn and that make you a desirable employee. What are yours? List your "good ats" that could move a task toward completion. Here are a few examples to get you started:

"I am good at getting people to follow my directions."
"I am good at working collaboratively with others."
"I am good at performing nitty-gritty tasks."
"I am good at typing."
"I am good at coming up with new ideas."
"I am good at following orders."

Now do yours.

MY "GOOD ATS"

I am good at _____

I am good at _____

I am good at _____

I am good at _____

I am good at _____

I am good at _____

I am good at _____

I am good at _____

I am good at _____

I am good at _____

I am good at _____

I am good at _____

In looking for a new position or career, use this knowledge about your "good ats" to your advantage; don't automatically eliminate any class of jobs that you previously thought you were not good at.

The work that you've done so far in this section is going to be valuable to you once you've identified and found your new position. It will serve to help you keep that job, to make the most of your own potential, and to keep track of when, where, and how you may be inadvertently getting in your own way and subverting your own best interests.

PREDICTING WHAT YOU BRING TO A JOB

You have now uncovered much important information about yourself. You have a composite picture that reveals much of who you are and what you bring to a job. This exercise is a first effort at being a matchmaker between yourself and a suitable, rewarding job.

From the lists you made earlier of your career "hunches," choose three jobs and list them here. At this time, do not select a job that you feel strongly drawn to.

A. _____

B. _____

C. _____

Now go back and reread the written summary statements about yourself—about your interests, your potential difficulties, and your capabilities. You are going to use this material to predict the outcomes of being employed at Job A, Job B, and Job C. Start with Job A: _____. As you write, be responsive to these questions: What do you predict you will experience (using whatever you know or can imagine about the responsibilities and contacts and style of this job) were you to accept the position? In what ways would you succeed? What aspects of this job would feel good? Which would you find it hard to accommodate yourself to? What would you predict would be the personal and professional difficulties you would run into with this work? What aspect would be the most rewarding? The most frustrating? Would you last at this job? Why or why not?

As you begin this assignment, as you comment about your feelings and performance on Job A, keep yourself free from judgments about how well you're doing the assignment. Just go for listening to your hunches, based on the material you've just reread and can reread again and again if you wish. Unless analyzing and predicting are skills you've already developed, expect to miss some points, even to contradict yourself or to be unfair—either to yourself or to the job. What you're developing is a feel for two highly useful capabilities; in some fields, these are called "analysis and prediction," in other fields, they're called "diagnosis and prognosis." And since you're not looking for a score on this work, you can enjoy both your hits and your misses. Remember, anything worth doing is worth doing badly—at first. So here goes on your first try.

Job A: _____

_____

_____

_____

_____

_____

Before you get to your second analysis and prediction, which will be easier and have more impact than the first, take a few more minutes finishing up this task. If you did want this job, wanted it badly, what—in the light of your present analysis and prediction—would you recommend that you learn, change, develop, practice, etc. once you are hired? List the recommendations here:

_____

_____

_____

_____

_____

While practicing this skill, you're developing a surer sense of what can go wrong and what can go right. Go on to Jobs B and C with a conviction that you are steadily improving your ability to know yourself and plan your future.

Don't forget. After each analysis and prediction, add your list of recommendations to ensure success on the job.

Job B: _____

_____

_____

_____

_____

_____

_____

_____

_____

I'd recommend that _____

_____

_____

_____

_____

Job C: _____

_____

_____

_____

_____

_____

_____

_____

_____

_____

_____

I'd recommend that _____

_____

_____

_____

_____

INVENTORY YOUR JOB ACCOMPLISHMENTS

You will be hired because an employer believes you can help make a profit or a difference in his or her business. You will be hired because an employer will recognize that you, more than the other applicants for the job, will aid the company and add to its productivity or its prestige. So it is high time to rethink your record of employment, or community service, in terms of a history of achievements. In so doing, you will make yourself unique; you will make yourself a person in demand. You are not going to leave it up to prospective employers to figure out what jobs best fit you. You are not going to avoid defining your strongest accomplishments before even entering the job market. No! You are going to take stock of and get to know yourself as a successful results-oriented individual and develop a clear and concise statement of your accomplishments. Not only will you then be ready to present yourself proudly to future employers, you will nip in the bud any inadvertent tendency simply to base a current career decision on past decisions.

You can organize for this task in several ways. You can review all the important jobs you have held, breaking them down into the actual functions that you performed. Or you can start, not from job titles, but rather by looking at all your work experiences as activities that were either operational in nature or aspects of management functioning. Very few jobs have only management or only operational functions; the majority, regardless of their titles, include both types of activities. Some examples of management functions are selecting personnel, setting objectives, making policy, supervising the execution of programs;* some examples of operational functions include report writing, selling, designing equipment, training personnel, keeping the books.

When you are interested in moving up in your established field, you will have a good sense of the needs of prospective employers. In these cases, your statement of accomplishments must attempt to meet those needs and desires, to address the priorities and particulars of the position you are seeking. If you are changing your field of specialization, you will need to generalize your accomplishments more, so you can sell your capabilities in a way that may be interpreted more broadly, rather than sell only your specific background.

To the extent possible, frame your accomplishment statements to support the level and type of position you are seeking. If you want a management position, pull from your past experience those accomplishments that support management activities. If you want an operational job, pull from your past experience those accomplishments that show that you directly added to productivity, or efficiency, or growth in your organization.

As you review some of the tasks and functions that you have performed, you will find that each has produced more than one result. If in performing some particular duty you had two or three accomplishments, then compose two or three accomplishment statements, each focusing on a single achievement. For example, your experience and skills in interpersonal relations and motivation may have resolved a situation full of hostility and conflict. As a result of your efforts, you may have (1) reduced conflict, (2) increased profit, and (3) aided in the fulfillment of contract obligations. These are three distinct results; write three separate accomplishment statements.

A well-formulated accomplishment statement is composed of:

1. What you actually did in a given task, job, etc., and what steps you took to perform this work.

* For a further definition of management activities, see Appendix 1.

2. How your employer benefited from this action. What the outcome was.

The following are samples of actions and outcomes most frequently included in accomplishment statements:

Actions	*Results*
Developed marketing and sales strategies.	Increased profit.
Designed and implemented sales training program.	Increased sales.
Reorganized bookkeeping systems throughout branches.	Reduced costs.
Performed market-research survey.	Enlarged market.
Designed new quality control system to measure quality.	Improved product quality.
Performed needs assessment, and designed, wrote, and implemented training program.	Improved teamwork and other interpersonal relations.

First *state the action* and then *describe the result*. The following list of action verbs will aid you in preparing your statements. Use this list to jog your memory about your many accomplishments and to help you make certain to state the action you undertook that enabled you to achieve the result.

ACTION VERBS

Accelerated	Converted	Executed
Accomplished	Coordinated	Expanded
Achieved	Created	Formulated
Added	Delivered	Founded
Analyzed	Demonstrated	Generated
Approved	Designed	Halved
Broadened	Determined	Headed
Built	Developed	Identified
Changed	Devised	Implemented
Clarified	Directed	Improved
Completed	Doubled	Increased
Conceived	Earned	Initiated
Conducted	Eliminated	Innovated
Consolidated	Established	Instituted
Controlled	Evaluated	Introduced

Invented	Researched	Traced
Launched	Resolved	Tracked
Led	Revised	Traded
Made	Scheduled	Trained
Maintained	Selected	Transferred
Managed	Serviced	Transformed
Motivated	Set up	Translated
Negotiated	Simplified	Trimmed
Operated	Sold	Tripled
Organized	Solved	Turned
Performed	Sparked	Uncovered
Planned	Staffed	Unified
Prepared	Started	Unraveled
Processed	Streamlined	Utilized
Programmed	Strengthened	Vacated
Promoted	Stressed	Verified
Proposed	Stretched	Waged
Provided	Structured	Widened
Purchased	Succeeded	Withdrew
Recommended	Summarized	Won
Redesigned	Superseded	Worked
Reduced	Supervised	Wrote
Reorganized	Terminated	

This is a crucial task for you to perform. It is worth whatever time and energy you put into it. The rewards are twofold. First, you will be surprised to find out how much you have already accomplished in your life. Regardless of your overall evaluation of previous jobs—whether they seemed pleasant or unpleasant, whether you judged that you'd performed them well or poorly—you will likely be able to isolate a variety of specific and real attainments that are to your credit. Second, if by doing this task you discover that what you have achieved is not really the kind of work you want to do, you deserve to know this now so that you move away from a direction that does not suit you and into a niche that will fit you better.

Look over the following sample statements of your management and operational accomplishments. We have prepared them to help you get started and to remind you of the parallels in your own work. If you were part of a team that did something important, don't overlook your contribution. Be prepared to rewrite your statements several times—sharpening them, making them more precise and clear—so that any potential employer can easily grasp what you did and what that action achieved.

Sample Statements of Accomplishments

1. Installed a complete accounting system, by department, in a large agency; decreased operating costs by 25 percent.

2. Through a reorganization and introduction of a methods system, reduced rework, eliminated schedule delays, and tripled in-house manufacturing quality.

3. Designed supporting equipment and techniques for a new process that raised its product market potential from $50 million to over $200 million per year. Established a sales and service organization from scratch in the midwestern and eastern market areas; 75 percent of company sales now originate from these areas.

4. Instituted a wage and salary program tailored especially to improve morale while eliminating waste; reduced payroll by $1 million.

5. Initiated and directed a community services program that incorporated a complete training program for future public administrators and processed every citizen complaint or request.

6. Organized and trained a sales force for selected marketing territories that resulted in a 67 percent increase in sales and profits.

7. Planned and implemented an office filing system for a law firm; reduced the time required for locating information by 25–50 percent.

8. Set up a bookkeeping system that reduced the amount of time to prepare payroll by 60 hours.

9. Initiated a volunteer fund-raising campaign and brought in $150,000 more in contributions than all previous directors.

10. While a college student, was elected to the student council and was instrumental in establishing council policies that resulted in better communications between faculty and students.

11. Significantly contributed to the writing of new curriculum manuals for high school English, broadened the scope of student interest, resulting in a diminished truancy statistic.

12. Doubled the number of homes available to American Field Service students in our community by writing a series of articles depicting the rewards available to families welcoming these foreign students into their lives for a year.

13. Remodeled and redecorated our home, which was then chosen for inclusion on the city's Tour of Beautiful Homes to benefit the city's restoration fund.

14. Created and managed a many-faceted program that honored individual differences, enabling 28 children of varied talents, backgrounds, and temperaments to meet and surpass the standardized academic requirements.

15. Created and implemented an employee training film library to upgrade the skills of 75 staff members. Results revealed that 100 percent of staff used services, which increased their training skills by 75 percent.

16. Resolved conflict-management problems with departmental employees. Devised a communications network to redefine work priorities and goals. Reduced tensions and increased productivity.
17. In an eight-month period, mastered the German language, which allowed the German-speaking project team to relate effectively to management and attain project objectives within prearranged time parameters.
18. Negotiated a $10 million property lease contract with a Fortune 500 corporation; improved gross revenues for owner by 25 percent.
19. Reorganized the management operations for several medium-sized companies. Increased revenues by 35 percent; decreased operational costs by up to 25 percent.
20. As regional vice president for a property management firm, operated 445,000 square feet of office space, plus two hotels and a private club. Annual revenue of these operations exceeded $4 million annually, resulting in management fees in excess of $200,000.
21. As a member of SHARE, Inc., planned several promotional and publicity programs to raise monies for charities. Raised over $550,000 in contributions ($5,000 raised first year). Over $1 million raised to date.
22. Coproduced a training manual on a known topic aimed at a new audience; responsibilities included layout, paste-up, research, and writing.
23. Created innumerable documents that conveyed management's position on key issues. Saved hundreds of supervisor hours in unnecessary communications.

MY SIGNIFICANT ACCOMPLISHMENTS

Review your work and other activities, and identify and list some of your most significant accomplishments.

1. _____

_____

_____

2. _____

_____

_____

3. _____

_____

_____

4. _____
   _____
   _____

5. _____
   _____
   _____

6. _____
   _____
   _____

7. _____
   _____
   _____

8. _____
   _____
   _____

9. _____
   _____
   _____

HOW DO YOU SOLVE PROBLEMS?

When you apply for a job, the potential employer is interested in discovering more about you than *what* you have accomplished in the past. You also need to convey *how* you solve problems. To do this well, you need to zero in on the actions you have taken to perform in your previous jobs and the problem-solving skills you used to get the job done.

The exercise on the next page is designed to aid you in focusing on your unique problem-solving abilities. As you work through the exercise, you'll no doubt have some difficulty. The reason for this is probably that you have never thought of yourself in this way before. So please don't get discouraged.

This exercise is particularly helpful for those of you who are looking to make a career change or reenter the job market. When you begin job inter-

MY PROBLEM-SOLVING ABILITIES

List the key tasks, functions, and activities you have performed in your job, community activities, etc. that reflect your experience.	What were the actions you undertook to perform these tasks, functions, and activities?	What were the results achieved from your actions?	What were the skills you used to accomplish these results?
1.			
2.			
3.			
4.			
5.			
6.			

viewing, focus on explaining how you have solved problems and met challenges in other job environments in ways that can be utilized by potential employers. This is the needs–benefit connection that you must make before you can convince an employer that you can perform in a situation where you have little or no specific background.

POTENTIAL JOB TARGETS

Now that you have completed your list of accomplishments and have investigated what problem-solving skills, likes and dislikes, and strengths you possess that can be utilized in a potential job, go back and review your list of career "hunches."

Select three job positions that you now think hold the most potential for you in terms of utilizing both your interests and your skills. Select those that you are willing to make a serious effort to attain.

1. _____

2. _____

3. _____

These are your potential job targets. It's critical that you investigate these job targets to help you identify what tasks, functions, and responsibilities they comprise.

To begin your research, review the Directory of Occupational Trades referred to earlier and listed in Appendix 2. Go to the library and read books, periodicals, and other materials on the subject. Also, make appointments to talk to people in the field. Ask them questions about their work, such as what their problems are and what strengths, talents, and skills are required to do the job. As you gather this information, be sure to check it against your skills and previous job accomplishments. How do your accomplishments fit with the tasks, functions, and responsibilities of the jobs you are now researching?

Once you have completed the investigative work, you need to choose which of the three job positions you intend to pursue. When you've made this choice, you will then be ready to begin working on the next section.

Section 2

PACKAGING YOUR SKILLS

As you are probably aware, to achieve success in marketing a product or service in the business world requires that you have a marketing strategy, a sequence of steps designed to elicit a particular outcome. In this instance, you need such a strategy to market your most valuable product—you! We can draw a parallel between the steps in marketing products and those intrinsic to marketing you and your job skills.

Marketing Products	*Securing a Job*
Developing the product	Knowing strengths and interests
Packaging	Writing resumes
Advertising	Mailings, telephone calls, references
Selling	Interviewing, negotiating
Signing the contract	Accepting the job offer

You have been putting all your energy into product development, and you are now ready to begin the next phase toward securing the proper job.

In this section of your manual, we will address the packaging of you.

THE RESUME AS A SALES TOOL

A resume frequently makes possible or facilitates an interview, and without an interview you cannot expect a job offer. It may take as many as ten or more interviews to produce several job offers. To obtain these interviews, consider your resume as a sales tool, a presentation that merchandises the product—in this case, yourself—for the resume is a vehicle for summarizing who you are and what you have done. The key element that brings this summary to life is the result-oriented accomplishment statements. So, rather than spend countless hours writing and worrying over the structure and format of the resume, put your time and energy to productive use by following these simple ground rules:

Do's

- Make your resume easy to read, using concise sentences. Remember, the reader must remain interested throughout.
- Leave adequate space between lines. Sentences that are too close together are hard to read.
- Keep your resume short. You may have to write several drafts. A two-page resume is optimum, but three pages is not uncommon.
- Stress your past accomplishments and the skills you used to get the desired results. Your accomplishments statements must grab the reader.
- Quantify the results of your accomplishments. Did you increase profits? By what percentage or dollar amount? Did you save the organization time and money? How much?
- Focus on information that is relevant to your own career goals. If you are making a career change, stress transferable skills to support your new career objective.

Don'ts

- Do not include a photograph of yourself.
- Do not use odd-size paper or loud colors. White, buff, and beige are appropriate colors for resumes. Be sure the paper is of good quality.
- Do not list previous salary history or reasons for leaving previous positions.
- Do not include references to areas of your life that have nothing to do with your current career goals, such as hobbies, membership in outside social organizations and military service that is not business related, names and ages of children, and maiden name.
- Do not go to a professional resume writer. Do your own. You know you better than anyone else.
- Do not have unreal expectations of what a resume can do. Do not expect

someone to hire you because of your resume. Use other tools for self-marketing, such as a broadcast letter.*

When you are ready to write your resume, review the samples on the following pages. There are two styles—the work experience resume and the skill-based resume. Choose the style that suits you best.

Know your own needs and objectives before selecting a resume style. If you are (1) changing jobs within the same organization or within your industry; (2) seeking upward mobility and more responsibility in a similar career plan; or (3) currently employed with a steady work history with no unexplainable gaps, then use the work experience resume style. This style simply lists your employment history, beginning with the most recent position and working backward. It is not necessary to go further back than ten years. This style will deal more with the content of your work, which will be familiar to the potential employer. You can insert accomplishments in this style resume if they are geared to the specific title you held.

As shown in Figures 1 and 2, the work experience resume contains the following information:

1. *Identification.* List your name, address, home telephone number, and work telephone number.

2. *Employment Objectives.* Use short descriptive phrases (e.g., Sales Manager, Cost Accountant, Sales Research Analyst, Research Psychologist, Social Services Administrator, Office Manager, Technical Writer).

3. *Background Summary.* List general functions and responsibilities which you have performed during your career that support your employment objective.

4. *Business Experience.* List employers in chronological sequence, starting with the most recent. List dates of employment, name and address of employer, your title, a brief description of your general responsibilities, some specific key functions you accomplished, and three or four significant accomplishments that support your job objective. Give this information for each job you have held during the past 10–15 years that is directly relevant to your present job objective.

5. *Previous Experience.* Provide a general statement of your less recent experience or experience that is not directly related to your current job objective. Emphasize any accomplishments and duties that support your job objective.

6. *Education and Training.* List degrees earned; dates are not critical. Also, list all courses taken that support your job objective. For jobs that do not require a college degree, itemize your education in full. If the job you are seeking requires a college degree and you don't have one, leave this section out of your resume or indicate the number of years you have completed.

---

* Such letters are used to market yourself to a large number of companies; broadcast letters will be discussed later in the manual.

7. *Personal* (Optional). List marital status and health status (only if good to excellent). Height and weight are not necessary. Leave date of birth or age out if you feel it will be a possible negative in the eyes of the reader.

8. *Professional Associations* (Optional).

9. *Publications* (Optional).

If you (1) are making a career change; (2) have a short work history; (3) are currently unemployed; (4) are entering or reentering the job market (first or second career); or (5) have been recently separated from the military, use the skill-based resume style. This style will allow you to stress skills that are transferable and will keep the reader from getting too involved in the content of your responsibilities with previous employers. You can play up your accomplishments (both work related and not work related) and play down your experience or lack of it.

Figures 3 through 6 show ways to incorporate the following elements into a skill-based resume.

1. *Identification.* Place your name, address, and telephone numbers (home and work) at the top of the page.

2. *Employment Objectives.* State briefly and clearly.

3. *Background Summary.* List general responsibilities and job functions you have performed during your career that highlight your strengths and problem-solving capabilities.

4. *Significant Accomplishments.* List five to ten significant accomplishments in your field of expertise. Be concise.

5. *Business Experience.* List dates of employment, titles held, and companies. (Leave out contents.)

6. *Education and Training.* List degrees, college or university, and courses taken that support your objective.

7. *Personal* (Optional). Marital status, health status. Leave out date of birth or age if it may have negative connotations.

8. *Professional Associations* (Optional).

9. *Publications* (Optional).

FIGURE 1. Sample work experience resume.

Robert Weston   Home Phone (713) 834-8042
12 Rochester Ave.   Message Phone (713) 834-7979
Marble Falls, Texas

OBJECTIVE: EDP Project Manager; MIS Director; Internal EDP Systems Con-
                sultant.

SUMMARY: • Twelve years of EDP management in petroleum, insurance, and
                  application software industries, preceded by assignments as pro-
                  grammer, systems analyst, and project leader.

                • Systems experience includes feasibility studies, proposal prepara-
                  tion, user requirements analysis, software evaluation, and system
                  design, development, and installation.

                • Management experience includes planning, staffing, budgeting,
                  performance evaluation, salary administration, and training.

                • Applications include accounting; benefit plans; financial, insur-
                  ance, management information; marketing; order entry; and pay-
                  roll/personnel.

EXPERIENCE:

April 1972   Apex Life Insurance Co., Dallas, Texas.
to Present   Manager, Group Insurance Systems

                Responsibilities involve administrative and technical direction of
                several project teams developing computer systems to support
                group insurance operations. Environment is IBM 370/168
                SVS/MVS, COBOL, TSO. Some significant accomplishments are:

                • Created department of 35 EDP personnel with group insurance
                  expertise from a project team of three.

                • Directed development of a large, integrated data base system
                  from inception to installation, a 60-man-year effort.

                • Developed a delinquent premium system that reduced delin-
                  quency rate from 25% to 3%.

                • Evaluated four data base management systems (TOTAL, IMS,
                  ADABAS, SYSTEM 2000) and acquired IMS to use in develop-
                  ment of the group insurance system.

                • Introduced top-down design and structured walk-throughs and
                  testing to ensure design integrity and to maximize productivity.

April 1969 to April 1972	Apex Software, Inc., Dallas, Texas. Vice President, Research and Development

Responsibilities included financial planning and control, produce planning and development, software package evaluation and acquisition, and technical sales support. Significant accomplishments:

· Development of a payroll/personnel computer system to be marketed nationwide.

· Development of a systems consulting capability to improve corporate cash flow.

June 1967 to April 1969	Esso Systems, Inc., Baytown, Texas. Assistant to Department Head, Operations Research and Systems Department

Joined organization as a Programmer and was promoted to Systems Analyst, Project Leader, and Section Head. Upon major reorganization, was promoted to Assistant to Department Head. Environment was IBM 7080, 360/50/65 OS, COBOL, and RCA 3301.

Responsible for interdivisional project planning, staffing, budgeting, and training. Acted as Systems Advisor to four divisions consisting of 100 professional systems analysts and operations research analysts. Accomplishments included:

· Prepared and obtained approval for first consolidated budget of $3.2 million for new organization.

· Developed a two-week in-house systems analysis training course.

· Consolidated the efforts of two newly merged groups to provide complete service to their customers.

· Directed the development of a financial reporting system used throughout the corporation.

· Built modeling capability into a sales profitability reporting system, enabling company to evaluate alternatives when normal supply sources were disrupted.

· Automated compiling and testing procedures for programmers to reduce operational set-up time and to standardize written instructions.

EDUCATION:	B.S. Business Administration, University of Texas; M.B.A. Statistics, New York University, Graduate School of Business, 1967
PERSONAL:	Married, excellent health

FIGURE 2. Sample work experience resume.

JOAN SINGLETON

140 W. 61st Street
New York, New York 10020
Home Phone: (212) 586-3401

Objective: Research Psychologist

Background Summary: Participated in several research projects involving intrapsychic and interactional themes. Leadership role in curriculum development for Smith College Psychology Department.

Experience:

Jan. 1978–present	Smith College, Northampton, Mass.
	Instructor—Teach courses in mythology and astrology, incorporating psychological perspectives.
	Head of the Curriculum Development Committee; developed a program of study which highlighted opportunities for students to participate in ongoing research projects.
Sept. 1976–present	American Society for Psychical Research, New York, N.Y.
	Assistant Researcher—Collect data in ganzfeld (sensory deprivation) biofeedback experimentation on psychokinesis. Substantiate general hypotheses with precision statistical evaluations.
1975–1976	Veterans Administration Hospital, Northampton, Mass.
	Health Care Intern—Developed recreational therapy program for geriatrics ward. Supervised volunteer programs in occupational therapy. Initiated new volunteer program involving the community in several therapeutic programs. Program still in operation at the present time; involves several hundred community residents.

Previous
Experience: Lab Assistant for Astronomy Department, Smith College, progressed from doing darkroom work to establishing coordinates for the telescopic photographic work.

Education and Training

Smith College, Northampton, Mass. B.A. in Psychology and Religion, January 1974

Duquesne University, Pittsburgh, Pa. M.A. in Clinical Psychology, 1976

Family and Children's Service, Braddock, Pa. In-service training and experiential fieldwork, 1974–1975

Gestalt Center of San Diego, La Jolla, Cal. Gestalt therapy training, certified, summer 1976

Maimonides Medical Center, Brooklyn, N.Y. Internship with Charles Honorton, research work in psychokinesis and clairvoyance, January 1976

Personal: Single, 27, excellent health

Professional Associations:
Association for Humanistic Psychology
Association for Transpersonal Psychology
American Society for Psychical Research
Association for Research and Enlightenment

FIGURE 3. Sample skill-based resume.

G. WILLIAM CARMICHAEL

#35 Westover Road   Home Telephone (213) 354-1212
Los Angeles, California 90017   Work Telephone (213) 362-1444

Objective: Data Processing Management

Background Summary: Fourteen years of experience in using systems to solve business problems. Experience features planning and developing major on-line systems, directing professional staffs of up to 200 people, and budget accountability up to $9 million.

Significant Accomplishments:

- Planned, organized, and controlled a $5 million division with a staff of over 100 people. Significantly improved company's profit position by responding to user–client needs.

- Developed five-year business plans. Resulted in company obtaining $3 million of new business.

- Reduced costs by $600,000 annually through installation of a multimillion-dollar consumer finance on-line system.

- Designed, developed, and administered comprehensive and detailed management audit programs for industry-wide usage. Reduced costs by 35%.

- Designed and developed major marketing programs for management audits and financial systems. Significantly reduced management review time and saved $224,000 per year in man-hours.

- Directed and managed large EDP organization, including planning, systems design, programming, operations, and support administration.

- Developed and installed manual systems utilizing industrial engineering techniques.

- Planned and implemented large-scale, on-line real-time, multiterminal computer systems.

- Controlled $4 million budget. Set up and operated regional accounting, including automated wage and salary program.

- Established $3 million Information Systems Division. Determined staffing requirements and implemented a full recruiting program, including advertising, interviewing, and personnel orientation.

Business Experience:

1/73 to Present	Vice President Systems Development	Great Western Bank Los Angeles, California
7/69 to 1/73	Director Plans and Programs	Alpha Systems Greenwich, Connecticut
9/66 to 7/69	Director EDP Consulting Services	Valle Corp. White Plains, New York
6/63 to 9/66	Manager Data Processing	Money, Inc. Newark, New Jersey

Education and Training:

St. Peters College, Rochester, New York
B.S. Business Systems

Personal Data:

Married
Excellent health

Professional Associations:

Data Processing Management Institute
Association for Systems Management

FIGURE 4. Sample skill-based resume.

Joan Englebert

7 Bay Street
Houston, Texas 77025
Home: (713) 678-5940
Work: (713) 278-9349

Career Objective: Volunteer Coordinator

Accomplishments:

Selling: Variety of successful recruitment efforts: 20 volunteers for educational census, 6–8 families per year to provide homes for foreign exchange students. Successfully persuaded skeptical admissions committee to accept minority students.

Planning: Helped plan and coordinate mailing of 50,000 promotional pamphlets for political campaign; designed and implemented system for recording information tallies and assigning territories to canvassers; planned and shared in supervision of volunteer-run educational census; was influential member of committee to design and implement training of Welcome Wagon volunteers.

Coordination: Coordinated center-city leaflet distribution for a political campaign; directed efforts of 42 political street workers; determined match between Welcome Wagon needs and volunteers' skills and interests.

Experience:

                1969–present: Welcome Wagon volunteer recruiter and trainer.

                1973–1978: American Field Service, Homes Chairwoman.

                1975–1977: Educational census worker, Des Plaines, Ill.

                1967–1972: Member, committee to elect city councilmen.

                1958–1960: Secretary, Pomeroy Pharmaceuticals, Clifton, Pa.

Education and Training:

                B.A., Beaver College, Glenside, Pa., 1958.

Personal: Single, free to travel.

FIGURE 5. Sample skill-based resume.

Joan Englebert

7 Bay Street
Houston, Texas 77025
Home: (713) 678-5940
Work: (713) 278-9349

EMPLOYMENT OBJECTIVE: Office Manager

BACKGROUND SUMMARY: Eighteen years experience in planning, supervising, developing systems and procedures, and interviewing.

ACCOMPLISHMENTS:

• Helped plan and coordinate mailing of 50,000 promotional pamphlets and coordinated center-city leaflet distribution for a political campaign.

• Designed and implemented system for recording information tallies and assigning territories to canvassers.

• Planned and shared in supervision of volunteer-run educational census; coordinated efforts of 42 street workers; my efforts increased the percentage of homes covered from 62 to 82%.

• Under high pressure for short-term census deadline, mediated conflict among staff members; helped achieve amicable compromises and boosted volunteer morale.

• Interviewed and selected volunteers for organization; determined match between volunteers' skills and interests and organization's needs.

• Was strong member on committee to design and implement training of volunteers.

EXPERIENCE:

1969–present: Welcome Wagon volunteer recruiter and trainer.
1975–1977: Educational census worker, Des Plaines, Ill.
1967–1968 and 1971–1972: Member, committee to elect city councilmen.
1958–1960: Secretary, Pomeroy Pharmaceuticals, Clifton, Pa.

EDUCATION: B.A., Beaver College, Glenside, Pa., 1958

PERSONAL: Single, free to travel.

FIGURE 6. Sample skill-based resume.

ANITA SUMMERS

22 Shepherd St.   Home phone: (212) 839–6748
New York, N.Y. 10017   Business phone: (212) MU3–2842

Career Objective: Public Relations Manager

Background Summary: Varied experience and success in oral and written communication to effect change; effective community outreach.

Accomplishments:

Communications   Repackaged high school history textbooks to make them capture the attention and response of a potentially resistant audience—students; this series has become a standard text in 42% of secondary schools in the Midwest.

Represented Little, Brown on "AM America," talking about women in publishing; station received 160 calls requesting copies of the interview and list of publishers.

Mediation   Spokeswoman for female staff at Little, Brown; resulted in effecting pay increases to bring women's salaries up to par with men's.

As spokeswoman for women at Little, Brown, represented them in their expression of concerns; prevented polarization of hostilities between staff and management.

Management   Coordinated speaking engagements for newly published authors.

Increased production level in copy-editing department by streamlining scheduling and hiring policies of outside resource people.

Experience: 1975–present:
Little, Brown, Inc., Manager, Copy-Editing Department

1970–1974:
University of Chicago Press, Editorial Assistant, Copy-Editing Department

Education: Bachelor of Arts, Marymount College, N.Y., 1970

Personal: Single, excellent health

Section 3

ADVERTISING
YOUR SKILLS

PREPARING YOUR ADVERTISING CAMPAIGN

A nationwide survey conducted by the Department of Labor in 1975 uncovered the following:

48 percent of job applicants find jobs with the help of friends or relatives.
24 percent find work through direct contact with employers.
13 percent use a combination of all the methods listed here.
6 percent obtain jobs through school placement services.
5 percent get jobs through answering help-wanted ads.
3 percent find jobs through public employment agencies.
1 percent find jobs through private employment agencies and search firms.

The message here is clear: you must use your own resources to get the job you want. At least 80 percent of your effort should be focused on the "hidden job market," which consists of those positions that are not advertised but are filled by "word of mouth."

So, although four alternative courses of action are open to you in advertising yourself, and you have the choice of selecting only one, your best move is to pursue all four to obtain the maximum number of job offers. The chart below lists these courses of action by priority in terms of the best rate of return (i.e., the most job offers) for the effort expended. To begin, mount an all-out effort to contact personal and business acquaintances as well as to contact business firms. While it sometimes pays to respond to ads or send your resume to search firms and employment agencies, these approaches are long shots; they offer the lowest rate of return for your efforts.

Priority	Course of Action	Probability of Interview and Job Offer
1	Personal and business contacts	Best
2	Corporation/business approach	Good
3	Newspaper advertisements	Fair
4	Executive search firms and employment agencies	Least productive

Only one in five jobs is advertised or listed with employment agencies or search firms. How come? Because employers fill most vacancies with friends or with people recommended by their friends. Also, the large majority of openings are filled by people who have made direct contact with the prospective employer, often without prior knowledge that the employer actually has a job opening.

Employing Your Personal and Business Contacts

Most people find their jobs through contact networks. Begin setting yours up, and consider these contacts your most powerful resource. Use them wisely.

Before you start building and using your contact network, complete these steps:

- Set up a card file or other system for keeping track of each phone call, letter, interview, follow-up, and promise. Without this, you run the risk of losing control of this resource and missing opportunities.
- Have a supply of updated resumes on hand.
- Decide what sort of help you need from various types of contacts:
    Information about a company or industry.
    Names of other contacts.
    Referrals to decision makers.
    Letters (or calls) of introduction.
    Advice on your campaign.
    General awareness of your availability.

Developing a network.   Make a list of everyone you know who would or could be potential contacts for you. These are not necessarily people who can hire you but who will serve as resource people or can direct you to decision makers.

Your list can include your immediate friends, past acquaintances, and people you have worked with or for. Don't forget your doctor, dentist, insurance agent, and other service-related professionals—they have other clients besides you. Drag out your Christmas card list and scan it thoroughly for other potential contacts.

Spouses of your friends and acquaintances are additional potential resource people for your network. Members of associations or organizations you belong to are also. You might even consider joining an organization in your field of interest.

When you start listing your contacts, your memory will be jogged and more names will come to mind.

This contact list becomes your direct list—people who know you well and those who at least know you casually. You can go to them directly. These contacts can rarely offer you a job, but they can become part of your network and introduce you to others who can hire you.

Your *indirect* list will be made up of referrals that you have gotten from your direct list. These contacts form the bridge between you and the decision makers in your target companies. This is a much more effective way of gaining entree to these companies than writing letters or even meeting personnel people. The decision makers will often be aware of their personnel needs long before an official job opening is declared. Thus, developing a contact network is an important way of tapping the "hidden job market."

Using your network. When your contact list is ready, then get on the phone and start calling. Here are some approaches you might use:

- Tell your contact you are planning to leave your present company to seek greener pastures and would appreciate advice on your "marketing campaign."
- Explain what your broad career goals are and solicit your contact's views on their appropriateness.
- Ask for names of influential people in the industry or target companies you have selected.
- Say you will keep in touch periodically as your campaign unfolds.
- Offer to send a resume.
- Tell your contact what sort of help he or she might furnish.

Carefully record useful data and names that come up during the call. Do not ask anyone for a job. Avoid putting your contacts through the unpleasantness of saying "no" before you find out what help they can offer. If they think of jobs, now or later, they will bring them up.

Try to arrange a brief meeting, such as a lunch date or even a 15-minute interview with important contacts. The face-to-face discussion strengthens your ties with the contact. Save the guts of your message for your get-together; don't unravel it all in your first phone chat.

Don't hesitate to call people you know moderately well at home. They are likely to be more relaxed, and your call will seem more personal.

Sometimes an influential contact who is one of your boosters will be willing to write letters to high-level executives in your target industry or companies. This is "powerful medicine." (Be sure to request a copy, so you can follow up.)

Most of these people, though busy, will be willing to help you. Remember—

- People usually like to help a fellow human being.
- Many people have been in your same situation—or feel they might some day.
- They may be flattered by your request for counsel.

So your prime contacts are usually willing to comply with reasonable requests—for names, introductions, letters, and ideas. More important, they will tend to remember you when something of possible interest to you materializes.

For some of you, the first few phone calls may seem awkward or embarrassing. The best way to overcome this feeling is to plunge ahead. It also helps to:

- Make some notes about key things you want to say.
- Practice your opening lines on a tape recorder and listen to them played back.
- Get to your key points—your situation and your needs—quickly and directly. Don't circle around till your busy contact gets annoyed.

Broadening your network.   Each time you make a successful phone call or meet with a contact, try to elicit names of additional contacts—friends of your immediate contact, who may have still further ideas and other contacts. In this way, you can keep expanding your contact network, which greatly increases your ability to "penetrate the defenses" of your target companies.

In fact, if some of your contacts know your target industry or companies, show them your list of decision-making executives you are trying to see. Perhaps they will know an officer or board member and can get you just the type of introduction you want.

Following through.   Once you have established a useful contact, keep it evergreen by touching base every two or three weeks. Be sure to drop a note of thanks to those who go out of their way for you. And when you get relocated, write each of them a sign-off letter and thank you. Figures 7 through 10 show sample follow-up letters.

FIGURE 7. Sample follow-up letter to contact.

Mr. John Jamison
147 East Rose Blvd.
Buffalo, New York 00121

Dear Mr. Jamison:

I found it really exciting to spend time with you today, not only having the opportunity to talk with you, but getting a feel for a busy insurance office. I very much appreciate the time and the help you gave me. What we spoke of together and the sense I got of how your office ran only served to increase my interest in this new line of work. I know that I have the skills that are necessary to make a go of it. The help you provided by pointing out what parts of my background would be most useful to executives when they hire an office manager, as well as the leads you gave me, are going to be very useful. I intend to follow all of them up.

I'm excited by this opportunity and want you to know how I'm making out, so I'll let you know what comes of my calling the people you referred me to. Again, many thanks for both your time and encouragement.

Sincerely,

Leila Martin

FIGURE 8. Sample follow-up letter to phone contact.

Mr. William H. Johnson
1343 Front Street
San Diego, California 92101

Dear Bill:

It was so pleasant to catch up on events in your life on the phone today, and I very much appreciated your interest in my "coming events."

Your willingness to counsel and help is much appreciated, and I have given some additional thought to how I might take advantage of your kind offer.

In the immediate future, perhaps the most useful thing you could do would be to consider what is happening in our field and give me any thoughts that germinate regarding companies that are having a difficult time in marketing their commodities (in other words, outfits whose marketing techniques and skills are behind the times). For the moment, that seems to be the area in which I might be the most useful to a producer.

And then, of course, if you develop any hunches as to companies that have a need at the general management level, even though it might have to be reached through the marketing route, that would fit nicely with my ultimate career objective.

Meantime, I will begin to zero in on some target companies myself. I may call on you for the name of someone at the decision-making level in each company, so that I can seek an interview directly rather than through the personnel department.

As promised on the phone, I am enclosing four copies of my resume. If you decide to forward them to someone, I would appreciate knowing about it so I may be ready to respond.

Even though we haven't been in close touch in the last four or five years, Bill, I felt very good about our phone talk and want to say that you have given me a real boost—both in morale and in ideas for my "marketing campaign." You may be sure that any time I head West, I will look forward to a chance to drop in on you and admire your beautiful city.

Cordially yours,

Michael J. Remsen

FIGURE 9. Sample follow-up letter to contact.

Dr. Robert Mason
42 Park Avenue
Buena Park, California 92632

Dear Bob:

I want you to know how very much I enjoyed and appreciated our talk yesterday. I'm very grateful for the time and energy you took to help me; your counsel was useful and timely.

I've been rethinking my approach to finding the "right" position for myself—where I can be performing at my peak and providing an organization with top-notch work—and I agree that I would serve my own interests best were I to broaden my view of the types of industries I might fit into. So I'm taking some days to research the area and pinpoint, as per your suggestion, some additional companies, other than service organizations, that might well use my consulting skills.

This is clearly excellent use of my time, and I thank you for your insights that led me to this decision.

I'd like to get back to you when this task is done, to see whether you are familiar with any of these companies and their executive staffs. Should this be the case, I'd then appreciate an introductory call so that I can present my qualifications and interests to the most appropriate person.

For now, let me say again how good it was to talk with you, to experience your clear thinking and directness. Thanks.

Warmly,

Peter Lincoln

FIGURE 10. Sample follow-up letter to contact.

Ms. Ella North
323 Bush St.
San Francisco, CA 92141

Dear Ms. North:

I can't tell you how challenged and excited I was by the time you gave me this morning. That in 20 minutes you could have communicated so succinctly and attractively the opportunities in the public relations field was in itself a masterful example of effective communications. You were inspirational! I especially appreciate your having translated my initial interest in PR work into so much broader a vision of the kinds of impact someone in PR can make. I feel even more excited and look forward to putting my writing and communications talents to work.

So thank you. I intend to use what I learned today from your example, not only as I find a new job for myself, but as I exercise my new responsibilities. I hope that with your many contacts you will let me know if you hear of something that might be valuable for me to pursue. I would be very appreciative.

                                        Sincerely,

                                        Anita Summers

Researching and Compiling Information

Again, remember that the great majority of jobs are not advertised. To find these positions, you must develop an effective job search strategy. Once you've identified your fields of interest and potential job targets, you can begin to locate specific companies or organizations, and available positions requiring your skills.

The steps to complete this task are outlined below:

- Identify sources of information that you can use to develop a list of companies or organizations you may be interested in contacting to obtain your job objective.
- Investigate what the products or services are that these organizations make or sell.
- Determine what types of jobs or career positions these identified organizations have that would be of interest to you.
- Discover how these companies can use your skills and how you can best present your background to them.

You can find the names of companies and agencies in your field of interest through a variety of channels. Use your personal contacts; trade magazines; professional journals; newspapers; the Yellow Pages; trade, service or professional clubs; directories of corporations (see Appendix 2); business and professional associations (members' places of employment). Be resourceful; add to this checklist. List the companies and agencies in the space provided.

COMPANIES AND AGENCIES IN MY FIELD OF INTEREST

COMPANIES AND AGENCIES IN MY FIELD OF INTEREST

_____ _____
_____ _____
_____ _____
_____ _____
_____ _____
_____ _____
_____ _____
_____ _____
_____ _____
_____ _____
_____ _____
_____ _____
_____ _____
_____ _____
_____ _____
_____ _____

Now weed out from this long list you've compiled those organizations that are not suitable for you (or at least not on your preferred list at the present time) because of location, size, internal structure, salary policy, employee attitude, etc. Then find the addresses and phone numbers of the remaining organizations and also the name of someone who is sufficiently high up in the organizational structure to make decisions about hiring.

Some of your personal and business contacts will be able to provide you with information to help narrow down your list. The directories listed in Appendix 2 will give you locations, numbers of employees, and sales figures. Some information may also be gleaned by calling the personnel department of a company.

When you've accomplished this part of the job, prepare an index card like the one shown in Figure 11 and sequence, in order of priority, those companies you want on your target list. Then find out the name and title of the specific person you are going to contact.

In all cases, it is better to aim for the decision maker, the head of the department or section that attracts you, rather than the corporate recruiter or personnel people. Here again, the references listed in Appendix 2 will be invaluable, since these business directories list all officers and directors, along with their credentials and experience. In addition, you can use your network of contacts to find out who does what. Another rather simple and direct way is to call up the company and ask who is in charge of a given function and then get his or her full name, title, address, and phone number. If you've obtained your information through sources other than the company itself, you may want to verify it by calling the person's secretary or someone else in the company who knows who does what.

Add this data to the appropriate index card.

FIGURE 11. Sample index card.

INC International

1133 Sarento Road

Contact: Joe Minor, Sales Manager 243-8692

Date contacted	Method	Date of rely	Results
1. Sept. 9	Telephone call		Interview
2. Sept. 12	Personal interview		Referral
3. Sept. 15	Personal interview		Resume requested
4. Sept. 16	Resume sent	Sept. 20	Call from department head
5. Sept. 23	Interview		Job offer

(Front)

Data about This Organization and Specific Department

Sales department seems to be disorganized. Needs market research to identify target market for new product line to be introduced in 6 months. Sales down 30% from last year.

(Back)

Through your researching efforts, you have found out some information about each of your target companies that can help you decide the best way to approach a particular company. You will need to determine not only how your skills and interests make a good match with the company's need in general but, more specifically, how to highlight yourself in view of the fact that you're going after a job that has not yet (or at least not yet publicly) been identified.

The jobs in the hidden market exist in the sometimes shadowy form of business needs that have not yet been fulfilled. For example:

○ The job that should be created to better expedite the company goals.

○ The job that will be created to facilitate an expansion of the company in its present orientation or into new directions.

○ The job that will provide new leadership to the organization that is performing poorly.

○ The job that is needed to rescue the function that has fallen behind the growth of the business, either for lack of competence or of an adequate number of people.

○ The job that will be created when the new boss decides to "bring in his own man."

○ The job that will open up when an executive retires.

So, find out about the companies on your target list: what they do, how they do it, what they don't yet do that they might want to consider, how happy or unhappy their customers or clients are, etc.

CONTACTING TARGET COMPANIES

Now that you've chosen your target companies and know something about them, how do you make your initial contact?

Ideally, someone in your personal contact network will be able to provide the original entree for you by introducing you to the appropriate person in a company, making an introductory call, writing a letter recommending that a key person in the organization meet with you.

If no one in your network of contacts can do this for you, there are a variety of other suitable approaches from which you can select the most feasible for each company:

○ Writing a tailor-made self-marketing letter.

○ Sending mailgrams or telegrams to company executives.

○ Making a phone call to the decision maker you wish to interview.

○ Finding out the business or professional associations that the person you want to see attends and making contact at the next meeting.

○ Writing a personal "solution" letter to a key decision maker.

This last is an interesting approach that you may want to use if, in your researching of a company, you discover a particular problem that the company is trying to solve. In this instance, do some exploring on your own and look for possible solutions. Once you have come up with one, drop a handwritten note to a responsible manager, indicating to him or her that you understand what the problem is and that you have a possible solution to it that you would like to propose. Do not mention in your note that you are looking for a job. Allow this information to emerge during the interview, after you have had a chance to outline your solution to their problem.

In either writing a tailor-made self-marketing letter or making a phone call to the decision maker, the trick is to devise something to say in the first sentence or two that hooks the attention or provokes the curiosity of the decision maker you are trying to reach. This is where your creativity and your knowledge of the company (from your research work) come in handy. Here are some ideas for telephone approaches:

- If you work for a respected competitor or a well-known company, your title and company connection may get you an interview without your being too specific about what you want. You can perhaps get away with merely saying something like:

    "I'd like to discuss some marketing ideas (or technical problems) with you."

- Or you may suggest that the work you have done recently (in your field or function) seems so relevant to his or her company that you would like a few minutes to explore the possible mutual interest:

    "I've been working lately on the environmental aspects of new chlorine plants, and I'd like to exchange views with you."

- Or you may appeal to a special interest or personal involvement in some field:

    "Your talk on reverse discrimination at the convention last week fits remarkably with some work my firm is doing. Could I drop by for a few minutes next week and swap ideas?"

- Or you may be lucky enough to identify a particular need his or her company has.

    "I sense you are planning to expand in the importation of foreign auto tires. With my 20 plus years' experience in tire marketing, I feel we might exchange some useful ideas on how to accomplish this."

Your in is to suggest a need—business or personal—that you might help satisfy. Not *your* need (for a job), but a need of your potential employer.

Even if your target executives quickly sense that you are a job seeker, they may still agree to see you in the hope that you will bring them something they need—new ideas or an executive who can solve their problems. But to indicate that you are out of work and that you need a job is the weakest possible appeal.

Here are a few more examples of how to identify needs that you might satisfy:

"Mr. Smith, this is Janice Martin calling. I see that you are planning to open two branch offices in the San Diego area. I know that you will want them to be functionally effective and attractive and comfortable to work in. I have designed some esthetic and highly efficient offices for a number of firms in this area and have an abundance of ideas you might like to use. Can we get together so I can communicate them to you?"

"Hello, Mr. Smith. This is Jim Schwartz at Schering. I have helped Schering develop several of its most successful marketing campaigns, and I feel these same approaches could be very effective for your product line. I'd enjoy exploring the possibility with you. Could we get together for lunch next week?"

"Good morning, Mr. Smith. I'm Jess Wilkins at Maremont Optics. I've noticed you folks are moving toward supplying more of your own components, and I've spent several years accomplishing that at Maremont. I believe I could help speed up your transition. Could we explore the idea together some day next week?"

Although the above examples are for telephone contacts, the same principles can be applied to tailoring a letter to your target executive. Remember—

○ Put your "hooks" or attention-getters in the first sentence or two.
○ Appeal to the needs of your potential employer.
○ Make use of your present (or recent) title and company.
○ Shoot for an interview, soon. Promise to follow up by phone. Do so in three or four days.

Figures 12, 13, and 14 are examples of letters beamed at target companies.

FIGURE 12. Sample letter to target company.

Joyce F. Trudell
Dean of the College
Wells College
Aurora, N.Y. 13026

Dear Dean Trudell:

An uneaten meal nourishes no one. An unopened book teaches no one. Some meals are eaten and some books are read—these are the ones that have captured the attention of the potential consumer.

I know that Wells College has much nourishment and teaching to offer young women today. Declining enrollment is no reflection on the high purposes of the college but rather a symptom of inflated costs. I would like to help bring your institution to the attention of potential students and their parents as well as community leaders who need to know why Wells—its faculty and facilities—is a worthy investment in the future.

My background includes high-level communications skills—in writing, speaking, and marketing—as well as experience in effective community relations. I would like to explore with you the ways my talents and accomplishments can be combined to help Wells present its unique and valuable qualities to the public.

I will contact your office on Tuesday of next week to arrange for a time that would be mutually convenient to discuss how my background can meet the school's needs.

                                        Sincerely,

                                        Anita Summers

FIGURE 13. Sample letter to target company.

Jane Gorman
Niles Realtors
408 Juniper St.
Chicago, Ill. 78910

Dear Mrs. Gorman:

Some realtors sell houses. Some realtors sell property. Some realtors sell communities. And some really fine realtors know how to sell a way of life.

A really fine realtor knows how to qualify a buyer, how to sense the particular life-style that a customer is striving toward, and then how to match the customer to that particular home and property that will contribute to the realization of a dream.

I have developed some ways that make it easier to go underneath what people say they want in a house in order to determine what kind of a life-style they are really looking for. I believe this approach to knowing the people who come through your office and to serving them more effectively might be of value to you.

I would be pleased to talk with you about it. My knowledge of both houses and people has been cultivated over the past 18 years. I know houses inside and out. I know communities and what makes them tick. I know people.

If you would be interested in talking with me about these simple ways of reading people to facilitate the successful matching of home and buyer, I would be delighted. I will plan to call your office next week to make an appointment at your convenience.

Sincerely,

Joan Martin

FIGURE 14. Sample letter to target company.

Dr. Frank Balik
Vice President, Research and Development
Newmont Mining Co., Inc.
34 West Park Street
Greenwich, Conn. 06910

Dear Dr. Balik:

I am presently Director of Mining and Geology for International Minerals and have worked in this professional field most of my career.

Because our firm is gradually reducing its involvement in mineral activities, I have decided to seek "new pastures" where mining is a central and growing activity. Naturally, I have known about your company and its fine reputation and have taken a keen interest in your growth strategy, which has been so successful.

My special flair for combining technical insight with economic common sense could be useful to your company in view of the fact that Newmont is pursuing the new metallic find in Canada, which was divulged at your annual meeting last month. I would enjoy a chance to discuss with you how I might fit into your technical and business needs. Specifically, I feel that some of my own developments in beneficiating low-grade, nonmetallic ores could prove applicable in your own field of metallic minerals. Perhaps your new Canadian find will demand beneficiation because of its relatively low assay.

I will be in the East in the next week or two and will take the liberty of phoning you a few days ahead to see if we might spend a little while getting acquainted and sharing ideas.

Looking forward to the privilege of meeting you, I am

Yours very truly,

Dr. J. L. Otis, III
Director, Mining and Geology
International Minerals, Inc.

DEALING WITH THE DECISION
MAKER'S SECRETARY

Whether you are trying to reach your target executive by mail or by telephone, a secretary will probably stand between you and your target. There are a few executives who answer their own phones and open their own mail, but these are exceptions—especially at higher levels.

When answering the phone, some secretaries will find out your name and company connection and then put you through without further question. More commonly, however, it is their responsibility to find out what you are calling about and either put you off or redirect you to some other person or department.

To avoid being passed down the line is a real challenge to your charm and ingenuity.

One of the easy strategies is to say, "A mutual friend, Mr. Williams, suggested that I call your boss."

Or another approach is, "It's a personal matter."

If neither of these simple approaches does the job, then you may want to use the same logic and persuasiveness on the secretary that you had designed to use on the boss. In other words, let the secretary know what the topic of mutual interest might be and then assume that he or she has enough business savvy to judge if the boss truly might be interested.

Quite often, the secretary is not trying to be difficult but is just unable to locate the boss or put you through at the moment. Then, you should make every effort to maintain a friendly telephone contact with the secretary. Be sure to get the correct pronunciation and spelling of his or her first and last names. This will enable you, when you call back the second, third, and fourth times, to establish an amicable relationship that will eventually help you get through to your target executive.

If the secretary senses (or gets you to reveal) that you are a job seeker, he or she may suggest you mail a resume or telephone the personnel department. You may make the best of this situation, when you contact the personnel department, by saying that "Mr. Gordon's office asked that I contact you." But if you can make a reasonable case that your interest in the company is a nonroutine matter, then you may want to try a strategy along these lines: "Ms. Brown, the level of management position that would interest me is not usually handled by the personnel department but rather by a top manager like your boss."

None of the above techniques is particularly ingenious or foolproof. The real message is that, if you are persistent and sincere, the secretary who seems to be a barrier may eventually switch over to your side and then help you make the contacts that you seek. Keep trying. Be friendly. If necessary, make your sales pitch to the secretary, as if he or she were the boss. If you can find an excuse to drop in at the office in person, to deliver a handwritten note or to introduce yourself, this is often helpful.

Getting through by letter is somewhat more problematical, since you have no immediate way of knowing whether you have succeeded or not. One way to find out is to call the secretary of your target executive a few days after your letter was mailed and ask whether your letter has come to the attention of the boss. If the secretary is not sure, you might ask him or her to dig it out of the mail pile and bring it to the boss's attention.

In summary, keep in mind these valuable tips:

1. A mailing to individuals by name will always get a better response than a mailing to individuals addressed by title alone.
2. A well-written letter that emphasizes your previous accomplishments and the results you can produce for an organization will have more impact than a cover letter and a resume.
3. Envelopes marked "private" or "confidential" are more likely to reach key management personnel than are mailings without these notations. Also, if your envelope does not reveal your name and address, you will do better than if the envelope reveals the source of the letter.
4. Type or hand write your letters, depending on your familiarity with the person. Keep your sentences short and simple. Avoid flowery words, and be direct and to the point. Keep the paragraphs short. Indenting the first line of each paragraph or setting off each accomplishment in paragraph form will improve readability.
5. Avoid coming off as a "superperson." The best letters are the ones that are soft sell and emit confidence. Overselling can be just as disastrous as underselling.
6. The best time to mail your letters is on Saturday or Sunday, so that they will be received on Tuesday, the best day of the week for letters to hit your target audience in a corporation.

BROADCAST LETTERS

If you want to make contact with a large number of companies, one approach you can consider is the broadcast letter. This involves a mass mailing to a particular industry, geographical area, etc. These letters, like tailor-made letters, should go to individuals who have authority to hire. Expect only about 1 to 3 percent response from your mailing.

The broadcast letter has been used extensively by job searchers, with good results when properly designed. The purpose of these letters is to get the attention of the appropriate person so that he or she calls you into the company to discuss your capabilities. You must, therefore, motivate the reader to take action by enticing him or her with three to six of your accomplishments. Choose whether to structure your letter to fit a general field of endeavor or to tailor it to a more specific situation.

All the hints we gave you regarding tailor-made letters are applicable to this approach as well. In addition, if you are planning to run a large-scale campaign, we suggest you use a commercial typing and mailing service. If you choose not to use a mailing service, prepare all your materials in advance and then mail them out at the same time.

Remember—

1. Write a short, provocative opening sentence—either topical or accomplishment oriented.
2. Show how your capabilities can be of value to an employer.
3. List three to six accomplishments.
4. End with a suggestion for action. For example, "I'll be glad to discuss further details of my capabilities, as they relate to your needs, in a personal interview. I will telephone your office next week to arrange for an appointment."

Below are examples of introductory statements for broadcast letters:

"The purpose of this letter is to introduce myself and present my qualifications for the position of _____."

"For the past ten years, I have been employed as quality control manager for a Fortune 100 Company. My background includes: (list key tasks and responsibilities)."

"Is your company looking for an executive secretary with extensive experience in office management, excellent organizational skills, and superior skills in typing and shorthand? If so, I urge you to consider my credentials."

"During the seven years I have been in Chino State Prison—working as an internal auditor for the state of California. . . ."

"Spending four hours per day on the San Diego Freeway is insane. This is the reason I am looking for a challenging position as an administrator in Orange County."

"I possess expertise in budgets, directing and motivating people, training, purchasing, transportation, and program management. This experience was obtained working as a housewife for the past 15 years. I would like the opportunity to transfer these skills to your company as an office manager."

"I'm a young, bright, ambitious high school graduate with a burning desire to enter the field of production. I know you'll agree that I'm an excellent worker with high potential once you have given me the opportunity to prove myself."

"If I were you, I'd give serious consideration to my secretarial skills. My qualifications include typing (85 wpm), shorthand, an organized mind, two years of college, bookkeeping, and a strong dedication to achieve."

"I have been responsible for determining the real estate value of a city the size of Anaheim. As a property appraiser for 15 years, I am an expert in every phase of the business."

"Brains and a love for clerical work are my qualifications for the position of secretary. I'd like to talk to you in person about my experience."

If you decide to write a broadcast letter, review the samples shown in Figures 15 through 21 for some ideas.

Broadcast Letters Written by Third Parties

An executive who knows you well might be happy to send out a broadcast letter over his or her own signature (see Figure 22). Such a letter will have much greater power than your own, because most people believe that any responsible businessperson would not stick out his or her neck for you unless the writer is confident that you have the capability and talent to do the job.

FIGURE 15. Sample broadcast letter.

Dear _____:

In this day and age it's virtually impossible to find a bright, dedicated, and hard-working full-time bookkeeper who possesses a rounded experience in all phases of office management. I know, because I've tried to hire and train people with my background. It's tough!

Over the past 20 years, I have had a wide range of experience that encompasses preparing profit-and-loss statements, billing, credit and collection, tax preparation, payroll, and pricing. In addition to this experience, working for both small and medium-size companies in the advertising and sales fields, I possess excellent secretarial skills.

Some of my accomplishments are:

- Directed the financial affairs of a $3 million advertising company. Was instrumental in generating an after-tax profit of 15 percent.
- Set up and maintained an accounting department that handled over $5 million per year.
- Hired, trained, and directed the efforts of four key accounting clerks. Three have progressed to office manager's positions.

The above accomplishments are only a sample of my experience. I would be pleased to discuss my background as it relates to your needs, in a personal interview. I will call your office on Tuesday morning of next week to arrange for an appointment.

Very truly yours,

Richard Cavell
124 Stanford Lane
North Park, California 92111

FIGURE 16. Sample broadcast letter.

Dear _____ :

It's time to put my superior management and organizational skills to work in the service of adults. I am ready for a challenging administrative position with a human services organization. I recommend that you look at my record and consider me as the next addition to your organization.

For the past 12 years, I have been in a team-teaching position with the city of San Clemente. I have gathered experience not only in teaching but also in revamping tired curricula and reorganizing school personnel into effective and efficient teams.

In the course of this work, some of my accomplishments have been:

- Running a successful remedial reading program, while balancing the physical and emotional needs of students in a severely overcrowded school system.
- Creating a model of team teaching whereby communications networks were established and devising a system of group solution to problems.
- Designing an operational system to pool resources and talents in the development of the new program.
- Supervising teachers-in-training and conducting evaluation seminars that attracted a large percentage of the school personnel.

I would appreciate talking with you about how my skills could be put to use in your organization. I will call your office next Wednesday morning to arrange for an appointment.

Sincerely,

Luke Wills
731 Rosecrans Lane
Oceanside, California 92131

FIGURE 17. Sample broadcast letter.

Dear _____:

I have been involved for a significant period of time in the intelligent utilization of computers. My background is one of extensive electronic data processing (EDP) management experience in planning, organizing, staffing, training, and directing all disciplines and levels of personnel and equipment. I have had total responsibility for an organization of 116 people, a 15,000 sq. ft. facility, computer and office equipment, and an operating budget of $3 million. I am looking for an opportunity to utilize this experience in a new setting.

Contributions I have made include:

- Planned, directed, and completed the expansion of an existing data center by an additional 2,000 sq. ft. Resulted in the successful merging of two independent subsidiaries, reducing annual operating expenses by $138,000.
- Assumed the overall direction of a problem data center. In six months, the organization was functioning on schedule and within budget.
- Organized and directed the transfer of a large customer's data processing workload into an existing data center. Resulted in cost savings of $1 million per year.
- Planned and implemented a remote processing capability utilizing RJE devices. Provided full service to multiple locations. Increased yearly revenues by $1.2 million.

The above items are only a sample of my accomplishments. I would be glad to discuss further details of my capabilities, as related to your needs, in a personal interview. I will telephone your office next week to arrange for an appointment.

Sincerely,

Sam Mitten
321 NE 31st St.
Lecadia, California 92024

FIGURE 18. Sample broadcast letter.

Dear _____:

An uneaten meal nourishes no one. An unopened book teaches no one. Some meals do get eaten and some books do get read—these are the ones that have captured the attention of the potential consumer.

Your university has much nourishment and teaching to offer young people today. I would like to help bring your institution to the attention of potential students and their parents who need to know why your university—its faculty and facilities—is a worthy investment in the future.

My background includes high-level communications skills—in writing, speaking, mediation, and sales—as well as experience in effective community outreach. Here are some examples of my accomplishments:

— At Little, Brown, my task was to take a series of high school history books and, without changing an author's content, put a punch into the language so that the students would find the texts readable and interesting. The published texts were sent to schools throughout the Midwest, and many have become standards in the classroom.

— Also at Little, Brown, I was successful as spokeswoman and mediator for the female staff in my department in effecting pay increases that brought women's salaries up to par with men of equal experience.

— As a result of my appearance on TV's "AM America," where I was invited to talk about women in publishing, the station received 160 calls asking for copies of the interview and references for publishing companies to contact.

I know how to target the needs and interests of a specialized audience or clientele. I know how to communicate. I know how to capture interest.

I would welcome an opportunity to have an interview with you to detail more of how I see using my skills to promote your college. I will telephone your office next week to arrange for an appointment.

Sincerely,

Mary Lee North

FIGURE 19. Sample broadcast letter.

Dear _____:

Some realtors sell houses. Some realtors sell property. Some realtors sell communities. And some really fine realtors know how to sell a way of life.

A really fine realtor knows how to qualify a buyer, how to sense the particular life-style that a customer is striving toward, and then how to match the customer to the particular home and property that will contribute to the realization of that dream.

I have developed some ways that make it easier to go underneath what people say they want in a house in order to determine what kind of a life-style they are really looking for. I believe this approach to knowing the people who come through your office and to serving them more effectively might be of value to you.

Some of my accomplishments in sales and "matchmaking" are:

— In a foreign student exchange program, was instrumental in selling the program to a number of communities and in matching students with appropriate homes. As a result, the program grew from two homes provided in 1973 to ten homes provided in 1975, a level maintained today with new families participating each year.

— As a researcher and designer of kits for Welcome Wagon, selected marketing items that successfully matched the needs and interests of newcomers to the community. Resulted in a 30 percent increase in customer use of introductory offers and business coupons.

I have the background, creativity, and energy to help you increase both your sales and your efficiency in selling. I would appreciate the opportunity to talk with you. I will call your office next week to request a time that would be mutually convenient.

Sincerely,

Betty Ann Fields

FIGURE 20. Sample broadcast letter.

Dear _____ :

It's harvest time!

I have too much experience not to make it available in the service of a growing organization. It's time for me to reap the rewards of almost two decades of volunteer activity and time for you to reap the benefits of my experience and expertise as planner, supervisor, coordinator, manager, and problem solver.

Let me give you some examples of what I can do:

— As a volunteer in a city councilman's political campaign, I coordinated mailings to 50,000 townspeople, recruiting volunteers and supervising their work in this effort.

— In the Educational Census of 1975, I helped design the system for tallying all the data collected within the townships of Middlesex, Sommerchase, and Norwood. I was responsible for overseeing the work of 50 canvassers.

— As a mother of three and a housewife, I have had 18 years experience in budgeting and purchasing, coordinating schedules and chores, mediating internecine squabbles, and building teamwork.

— As a researcher and designer of kits for Welcome Wagon, I selected marketing items that successfully matched the needs of newcomers to the community, resulting in a 30 percent increase in customer use of introductory offers and business coupons. I was also instrumental in selling the Welcome Wagon coupon idea to 36 businesses in the communities of Fairfax, Littleton, Norwood, and Blimmton.

With these and other background accomplishments, a bachelor's degree from Beaver College, and early secretarial experience, I'm ready to translate my many skills to the business field. I would be pleased to discuss the details of my background, as they relate to your needs, in a personal interview. I'll call your office next week to arrange for an appointment.

Sincerely,

Betty Ann Fields

FIGURE 21. Sample broadcast letter.

Dear _____:

I have 18 years of profit-and-loss management experience in high-technology industries and an M.S. in engineering. My successful record in general management in line positions includes extensive experience in the mechanical, hydraulic, and electronic industries and recognized accomplishments in all disciplines of a production business, including turnarounds, start-ups, mergers, acquisitions, and foreign sales agreements.

As a group vice president with responsibility for seven divisions, I restructured the group to meet corporate objectives by doubling size and profits of one division by negotiating a unique sales/marketing agreement with a Japanese company, phasing out a division in a dying market without a loss, selling one at a substantial profit, and establishing a new division that grew to $3.5M in three years.

As a division manager, I increased profits of a $30M electronic components division from $3M to $4M within one year after taking charge, doubled the size of a military-oriented electromechanical division in four years by penetrating selected industrial markets with new products, and established manufacturing facilities in Puerto Rico for tax-free advantages and in Mexico for labor-cost advantages.

I have devised numerous innovative management techniques that have contributed to the above accomplishments. The following examples are applicable to most production businesses: development of a formula whereby sales personnel earn incentive compensation by maximizing profits rather than volume; installation of a unique "operator-involved" performance reporting system that improved production performance by 15 percent; evolution of a comprehensive managers quarterly performance review outline that has uncovered potential problems, improved performance to plan, and eliminated communications problems; compilation of a definitive paper outlining the management do's and don'ts necessary to achieve maximum return from acquisitions.

I would appreciate the opportunity to discuss the advantages of these management concepts as they apply to your operations. I can be reached at (714) 233-1214 or (213) 979-9120 during the upcoming week. If this is inconvenient for you, I will call you before the end of the month to arrange for an appointment.

Yours truly,

Sam Alterdice

FIGURE 22. Sample third-party broadcast letter.

Dear _____ :

I have learned in confidence that Mr./Ms. _____, who is presently employed as a manager of _____ at ABC Corporation, is seeking to make a career
change.

Prior to his/her present position, he/she had several years of experience with the
_____ Company and _____ Company. I have known Mr./Ms.
_____ for _____ years, both personally and professionally. I am impressed with him/her as an individual and consider him/her to be of high integrity,
with sound business accomplishments:

[List three to six accomplishments here.]

Mr./Ms. _____ is in good health and possesses a well-rounded education.
I am convinced that when you meet him/her you will agree with me that your organization would benefit from a person with his/her capabilities.

Please feel free to contact him/her at _____ and to use my name.

Sincerely yours,

John Copely

Responding to Replies to Your Broadcast Letters

Generally, you will receive a significant number of replies from the companies that have received your letters. The large majority will be polite rejections. Don't throw the letters in the trash. Review each letter and note the date of the letter and the name of the person who signed it. Record this information on your index card for that company. Next, sort the letters into priority areas (geographical, industry, etc.). There may be some companies that you are not interested in pursuing; if so, discard those letters. If you do not have enough information on each company to make a decision, go to the public library and do some further research. Then decide how you will reapproach those companies that interest you. The idea here is to begin to zero in on those companies and managers that you want to recontact and to plan your strategy.

One approach is to wait four to six weeks after you have received your rejection letter and write another letter to a specific person in the company (possibly the one who wrote you the letter of rejection). Three to five days later, call the person on the phone and seek an interview.

Another approach is to write directly to a manager whom you have identified from your research and indicate that you have received a letter from Mr./Ms. _____ telling you that there were no openings at the time, but you are still interested in the company and would appreciate being considered for a position when one becomes available. Again, after a reasonable time, call the manager on the phone to attempt to set up an interview. (Refer back to our advice regarding phone calls.)

If your broadcast letter is well written and strikes when there is a current need or potential job opening, one of three things is likely to happen:

1. The personnel department will mail you an application to fill out and return.

2. You will receive a telephone call from the company asking for more information about your job history and salary. If you pass the screening, the company may ask you either to come in for an interview or to submit a detailed resume.

3. You will receive a letter asking for more information and requesting you to send a resume and salary history.

STRATEGIES FOR COMPLETING
JOB APPLICATIONS

A job application is a screening device that may eliminate you from consideration even though you're a qualified applicant. Try to get an interview with the company first, and bring the application with you at that time. If at all possible, do not complete any application until after an interview. In this way, you can be more responsive to the job requirements.

Some application forms ask you to state the position you are applying for along with your second preference. If you have been invited for an exploratory interview as a result of your broadcast letter, you may not know exactly what the company has in mind. You should then leave these spaces blank.

If your application form offers limited space or opportunity for you to state your background in proper detail, attach a page listing your accomplishments. Provide as much information about yourself as possible.

Do not commit yourself to an expected salary. Leave the space blank or state "open." In the space provided for references, state that you will furnish names at a later date. You do not need to give your age or sex.

Complete the personal data sheet provided here and use it as a reference whenever you have to fill out an application. This will help you recall your work history and the necessary particulars that are frequently asked on such forms.

PERSONAL DATA SHEET

Name _____   Telephones: Residence _____

Address _____   Message _____

Employment Record

From/To	Company	Address	Salary
_____	_____	_____	_____
_____	_____	_____	_____
_____	_____	_____	_____
_____	_____	_____	_____
_____	_____	_____	_____
_____	_____	_____	_____
_____	_____	_____	_____

Education

School	Location	From/To	Diploma/Degree
_____	_____	_____	_____
_____	_____	_____	_____
_____	_____	_____	_____
_____	_____	_____	_____
_____	_____	_____	_____
_____	_____	_____	_____

References

Name	Address/Zip	Position	Phone
_____	_____	_____	_____
_____	_____	_____	_____
_____	_____	_____	_____
_____	_____	_____	_____
_____	_____	_____	_____

USING THE NEWSPAPERS AND JOURNALS

Answering Classified Want Ads

Newspapers throughout the country carry pages of advertisements for positions at all levels. In addition, business and professional publications often carry ads for job opportunities in specialized fields. It is a good idea to become familiar with these ads. Study them enough to get an impression of what kinds of jobs are available in your field and what sorts of baits the advertisers are using to get your attention.

To give you some perspective, a typical ad in the *New York Times* classified commonly draws 500–1,000 replies. Obviously, if you elect to answer one of these ads, your cover letter and your qualifications must be both attention getting and an excellent fit for what the advertiser has in mind.

Your chances of making good connections by answering ads are greater if the jobs are in a very specific or technical field that happens to be the same as your own. On the other hand, ads for such positions as general manager or marketing executive tend to draw so many replies that no matter what the field your chances are relatively small of even getting a reply. Our experience shows that only about one in a hundred letters written by our clients draws any reply at all. Therefore, this is generally a low-yield way to use your time.

There's an art to answering ads. Most job hunters fail to win in this arena because they don't understand the game they are playing. If you intend to use this marketing strategy, we recommend that you follow these guidelines:

1. *Read the ad carefully for content.* Underline the key words that describe the skills required.

2. *Prepare a rough draft of your response.* Attempt to read between the lines to determine the unnamed qualities needed; condition your response accordingly. Avoid clichés, and let the responsiveness and substance of your capabilities speak for themselves. Be sure, however, that you use the same key words in your letter that you underlined in the ad. The writer of the ad, who is usually an employee in personnel, has a definite pride of authorship. Thus, your chances of passing the preliminary screening will increase if you feed back the writer's words.

If the ad requires a particular degree of experience that is not quite in your background, go ahead and answer the ad anyway. As long as you are in the 75 percent range, you should qualify. Do your best to establish a sound and appealing needs-benefit linkup with whatever information is at your disposal. Remember, the objective of your ad response is to get the interview; your strategy is to give the reader enough of the right kind of information to arouse his or her interest but not so much that it precludes an interview and prematurely screens you out.

3. *Don't send a resume unless it fits the ad to a tee.* Even if the ad says you must send a resume and include a history of your earnings, don't do it. The game plan of the company is to get as much information from you as it can without providing you the same background about its position. This is the personnel department's way of screening you out before you have had a chance to get an interview.

Avoid responding to companies that don't identify themselves or give only a box number. Reply to advertisers that state the specific experience and skills they are seeking for the job. Don't give your age or salary level in your letter. If the ad states that you must give your salary history in order to be considered for the position, give your salary range.

4. *Hold your answer for several days.* Let some screening occur before your letter arrives. This decreases the probability that your letter will be rejected by the personnel department in the initial crest of responses.

5. *If the company gives a phone number and a contact person in the ad, call to request more information.* By telephoning the company or dropping into the personnel department before sending your response, you may be able to get more background about the position. In addition, try to identify the line manager who is hiring and what additional qualifications are required. If you are lucky, you may be able to talk to the hiring supervisor, thereby avoiding the preliminary screening process that occurs in personnel.

6. *Remember that the job market and its "mood" change constantly.* If a particular approach or style in answering ads doesn't appear to be working, try a new tactic. A periodic overview of current ads will enable you to spot trends and note changes in focus and content and to change your own approach accordingly.

Before you start to draft your response, take a look at the sample letters in Figures 23 through 25.

FIGURE 23. Sample response letter to an advertisement.

BCR, Inc.
4080 Front St.
Boston, Mass. 02213

Dear Sir/Madam:

I am delighted to tell you some of my accomplishments over the past eight years, since I believe they qualify me superbly for the position of Program Developer that you advertised in the *Boston Globe*.

My background includes high-level communications skills—in conflict negotiation, persuasive writing and speaking, and public relations—as well as experience in effective community outreach.

At Little, Brown, where I am currently employed, I served successfully as spokeswoman and mediator for the female staff in my department in effecting pay increases that brought women's salaries up to par with men of equal experience. I was able to prevent the polarization of hostilities between staff and management in this difficult situation by engaging common concerns and by my ability to translate the needs of women in terms comprehensible and persuasive to male administrators.

At this publishing house, I was responsible for successfully repackaging history textbooks by capturing the attention and response of a potentially resistant audience. As a result, this particular experimental series has become a standard in 42 percent of the secondary classrooms in the Midwest. I also designed and implemented a more cost-effective use of freelance copy editors.

I am familiar with your program both from newspaper articles and from personal exposure to individuals who have used your services, and I am impressed with your organization. I look forward to hearing in more detail about the full responsibilities of Program Developer and will be happy to meet with you to provide more data about my background and references. Please call me at (617) 772-3842.

Sincerely,

Lucinda Smith
1371 High Street
Boston, Mass.   02122

FIGURE 24. Sample response letter to an advertisement.

RCA Manufacturing
4444 Severs Road
Los Angeles, California 90057

Dear Sir/Madam:

I am submitting my credentials in response to your advertisement for a Manager of Manufacturing that appeared in the Sunday edition of the *Los Angeles Times.*

My work experience includes 15 years of manufacturing operations experience in the food, petrochemical, and plastics industries. My general responsibilities involve managing industrial engineering, research and development, purchasing, quality control, and transportation.

Some significant accomplishments in these areas are:

- Organized previously autonomous subsidiaries into a single operating group of three divisions. Increased efficiency 30 percent.
- Implemented a troubleshooting program for subsidiary manufacturing units to identify weaknesses. Turned units into a profitable, on-schedule operation in three months.
- Assumed responsibility for international manufacturing operations. Successfully implemented production schedules and initiated quality control standards that increased efficiency by 23 percent.
- Developed and controlled new production processes. Reduced man-hour costs by half. Saved $200,000 in labor expenses.
- Set up a critical path system that reduced production delays by 75 percent.

I possess a B.S. degree in industrial engineering and an M.B.A. degree.

I would be glad to discuss further details of my capabilities as they relate to your needs in a personal interview.

Sincerely,

Bill O'Connor
1046 Neptune
Seal Beach, California   90740

FIGURE 25. Sample response letter to an advertisement.

To Whom It May Concern:

    I am pleased to suggest myself to fill the position of Office Manager as advertised in the *Philadelphia Inquirer* of June 14.

    I have 18 years volunteer experience in planning, supervision, coordination, and conflict resolution. I am particularly effective in coordinating and problem solving and in being able to work effectively with people at all levels. In short, I would call myself a talented troubleshooter.

    Let me give some examples of what I can do:

— As a volunteer in a city councilman's political campaign, coordinated mailings to 50,000 townspeople, recruiting volunteers and supervising their work in this effort. Candidate was elected.

— In the Educational Census of 1975, designed the system for tallying all the data collected within the townships of Middlesex, Sommerchase, and Norwood. Task was completed on time and within budget.

— As a mother of three and a housewife, possess extensive experience in budgeting and purchasing, coordinating schedule, mediating internecine squabbles, and building teamwork. Family has grown into successful and prosperous adults.

    With these and other background accomplishments, a bachelor's degree from Beaver College, and early secretarial and administrative experience, I'm ready to translate my many skills to the business field and to make my talents available to industry. I'll be glad to discuss further how my many qualifications will mesh with the needs of your office.

Sincerely,

Rebecca Ridgely
1321 Evans Terrace
Philadelphia, Pa.

Placing Ads

Our experience indicates that results from placing position-wanted ads are exceedingly poor.

Checking the Personal Business News

As part of your campaign, watch the newspapers and journals that provide information on recently promoted executives. If you find someone in a company that interests you, call him or her up after a week or so. Congratulate the person on the new position and then let him or her know that you are available for a position in the company. If you follow this approach diligently, you will get interviews as well as referrals and job offers.

USING EMPLOYMENT AGENCIES AND EXECUTIVE SEARCH FIRMS

Employment Agencies

If you decide to contact employment agencies to help you in your job campaign, you need to know that they generally operate in one of three ways. You may be required to pay a fee to the agency, which will run up to 1–1.5 percent per $1,000 of the starting salary, payable upon placement. A second way agencies earn fees is to charge the employer for their efforts in locating and screening clients. The third method is to charge a negotiated fee, paid in part by the selected applicant and in part by the employer.

Be selective in your choice of an employment agency. If you do not know the reputations of employment agencies, try calling several personnel managers in the area where you wish to work and asking them if they can help you locate the best recruiting and employment agencies for people in your field of interest. As you obtain the names of these agencies, also ask for a name of a particular person in the office whom you can contact.

Once you have this information, make your phone calls. Indicate that Mr. Jones, the personnel manager of ABC Company, referred you. The job counselor will likely be flattered to have been recommended and this may help you get special treatment. Attempt to set up a personal appointment. Prior to going to the interview, prepare a list of companies you have researched that you would like the counselor to call for you to set up an interview. You may wish to select two or three job counselors in a given geographic area to maximize your efforts. Perhaps indicate to each counselor that you are leaving town for a week or two and that when you return you hope that he or she will have several interviews set up with people on your list. This system has worked for others and can work for you also.

It is wise to interview the job counselor with whom you will work to determine his or her experience and, in particular, familiarity with your field of interest. It's important that you "feel" compatible with the counselor you intend to work with and have a commitment from your counselor that he or she will work diligently for your best interests. Do not expect counselors to spend time trying to help you focus on a job objective. That's not the business they are in. They work on a quick turnover of applicants to jobs by looking for the "round peg" to fit in the "round hole."

Follow up with your job counselor every two weeks or so to check on the progress. If you are not receiving the service you desire, contact another agency to supplement your job campaign efforts.

Executive Search Firms

Executive search firms work by arrangement with client companies to fill positions with salaries of $20,000–25,000 and above. The search consultant is paid by the client company at a rate of 25–40 percent of the starting annual salary. Most search consultants specialize in a given industry and will cover a national area.

As a rule, executive search firms, or headhunters, work solely from resumes. They generally want to interview an applicant only when there is a specific opening or search assignment. It is worth trying to get interviews with search firms, however, particularly if you are unique or at a sufficiently high level that they can logically take an interest in you whether they have an immediate opening or not. Furthermore, the search firms are well tuned in to the job market and often know what's happening inside their client companies.

Knowing a member of the firm through a contact is a big help in getting an interview. Unsolicited phone calls often get brushed off, unless you are unusually persistent and ingenious. However, sometimes a walk-in call will get at least a brief courtesy interview, on the basis of which the firm will decide whether or not you are a "hot commodity." If your job level is high enough so that you have been, or might eventually be, a potential client, they are much more likely to grant these courtesy interviews in order to build up marketing goodwill for the future.

If you are chosen for an interview by one of the search firm's clients (and this is likely to happen only after being thoroughly interviewed by the search firm itself), then you've moved up into a leading position for a job opportunity. Search firms usually submit only two to three candidates. At this point, the search associate will want to guide your every move in a tightly controlled manner. He or she will want to know whom you are contacting and when and will want immediate feedback about how any interview or contact proceeded. One of the worst things you could do would be to try to bypass a search firm that has put you in touch with one of its clients.

The search associate usually knows the client and the job situation quite well, although there are deplorable exceptions to this rule. In any event, you can learn a lot about the company, the job, and the executive who is going to interview you by listening carefully to the search associate in advance. Make notes.

If you wish to contact search firms, send a resume and a cover letter. The cover letter should reveal in a concise manner the job you are seeking, the skills and experience you possess, your salary requirement, and the geographical location you desire. Figures 26 through 28 show sample cover letters.

FIGURE 26. Sample Cover Letter to Search Firm.

Dear Sir/Madam:

If you are currently attempting to fill a responsible public relations or corporate communications position for one of your clients, you may find the enclosed resume of considerable interest.

At age 32, I am seeking immediate relocation and advancement, having attained nine years intensive and broad-based experience in key PR communications functions. An M.B.A. degree and more than five successful years with a major corporation in the media center of the nation are among my credentials.

While I prefer to relocate outside the New York metropolitan area, I am primarily seeking an opportunity for growth and advancement in my field. I will give full consideration to opportunities in internal or external communications functions and in consumer, service, or industrial sectors. My current salary, with bonus, is $25,000.

I look forward to discussing specific requirements of positions with your client organizations and will respond immediately to your call. Please feel free to call me at my office or home.

Many thanks for your interest and consideration.
Sincerely,

Manuel Gomez
33 W. 89th St.
New York, N.Y. 10021
Home phone: (212) 877-8008
Business phone: (212) 582-8192

FIGURE 27. Sample Cover Letter to Search Firm.

Dear Sir/Madam:

Enclosed is a copy of my resume for your review against current client assignments.

I seek a position as a controller or vice president of finance with a small to medium-sized company.

My background includes 15 years of financial experience, 11 of which have been in the retail industry and 4 in public accounting. I am 37 years old and have a B.S. degree in accounting (B average) from Brooklyn College.

Should you be recruiting for a financial executive in the $25,000–30,000 salary range, please contact me. I would appreciate the opportunity of a personal interview to relate specific experiences that fit your needs.

Sincerely yours,

Elias Smith
3437 Northwest
Seattle, Washington 98122
(602) 323-6711

FIGURE 28. Sample Cover Letter to Search Firm.

Dear Sir/Madam:

    In your search assignments, you may have a requirement for a professional sales marketing executive with an outstanding record in both start-up and turnaround operations.

    Having progressed up through the ranks from salesman to vice president, marketing, my experience is with three companies of $100 million and up. Management responsibilities cover organizations of 10–250 people, with sales of $1.5–$35 million.

    Some of my accomplishments include:

- As part of a new management team at Burndy Corporation, brought a division from an $800,000 loss to a $1.5 million net profit in less than two years; during the 1974 recession, we increased corporate profits from 5 percent to 7 percent net—in spite of a 25 percent industry-wide drop in electronic connector sales.
- Started a new division for Bell & Howell, establishing them among the top three companies in microfilm equipment and system sales; it is now their largest and most profitable product line.

    The enclosed resume outlines my 26-year growth record. I am currently seeking a position as V.P. of marketing with an income of $35,000–45,000.

Cordially,

Burt Brown
121 No. 7th Street
Paramus, N.J.
(201) 311-1181

REFERENCE-CHECKING HINTS

In response to your letter, phone, or direct contact with future employers, someone may ask you for references. Unless you know what each reference will say about you, you run the risk of being hurt by the reference, even though the writer's intentions were good.

Therefore, we suggest that you write a reference statement and submit it to each person you intend to use for a reference. This is particularly important if you have been terminated, since your former boss may instinctively try to justify his or her action by emphasizing your alleged faults instead of remembering your years of solid contributions. It is also crucial when you are making a career change, since your references may inadvertently emphasize qualities that, though admirable, are not the necessary and pertinent qualities for the new position you seek.

Using the outline suggested below, try to put yourself in your bosses' shoes and write the best statement you feel they would be willing to make about you.

- Credibility: How does reference know you?
  - Example: "Joe reported directly to me for four years, and I was close to his work for the whole ten years."
- Accomplishments: What did you do well over the years?
  (List several)
  - Example: "In our housewares product line, Mary quickly assessed our marketing problems, developed a new approach, and helped get us out of the red."
- Personal Traits: "What kind of a person are you?"
  - Example: "Gwen is likable and honest. She is cheerful and straightforward."
- Weaknesses: Where do you need to improve?
  - Example: "Frances has a tendency to dive in and do part of her subordinates' work when the heat's on."
- Reason Why Left: What is the "official" story?
  - Example: "Charlie was brought in here to put us in the battery business, but we eventually decided not to go. That made his job dead end, and we agreed he could probably do better elsewhere."

Don't be afraid to blow your own horn. Use strong, positive words and phrases. The prospective employer will likely take your reference with a grain of salt, so try for an impressive, yet credible, statement.

When you've finished the statement, take the draft to each reference and ask if he or she is willing to say "these kinds of things" in answer to a phone inquiry. (Hardly anyone checks references by letter anymore.) Should your references feel uncomfortable with any part of the statement, offer to adjust that part of it until it is acceptable to them.

Then have the statement typed and give each reference three copies—one for his or her use at the office, one for use at home, and one for your reference's secretary or file.

Remember to keep the statement brief; a few short paragraphs will do. The listener is a busy person and so is the reference giver.

People to choose as references:

- Your ex-boss is an obvious choice, since he or she knew your work.
- A peer who worked closely with you can also be credible.
- A higher level boss is sometimes impressive, too, provided he or she really knows your work.

If your recent boss proves unable to speak well of you, try going back to an earlier boss. Avoid ancient references. Avoid too many references; three should be enough. Don't offer references until asked.

TIME MANAGEMENT ACTION PLANNING

Now that you have a clear job objective, have researched your target companies, and have written your resume and letters, it is time to develop a plan to manage your time and your job search campaign. The planning of your campaign is necessary to obtain your goal—the new job. This plan will be your program for success, so spend time developing a realistic plan with objectives that you can meet.

- Consider the major steps necessary to obtain results.
- Break each step into component substeps.
- Look ahead to foresee any difficulties that will impede your gaining results.
- Set priorities.
- Set a date for completion—the date you start the new job—as well as dates for each major step in your plan, and estimate the time required to complete each substep.

Review Figure 29 and then design your own personal action plan.

FIGURE 29. Sample of Time Management Action Plan.

1. Make personal contact with ten companies per week.

2. Visit five employment agencies per week.
   (a) Call companies in my field of interest at random and ask person-nel officers for suggestions of reputable employment agencies.
   (b) Check with my personal contacts to discover if any are familiar with these agencies and would give me letters of introduction.

3. Send out 25 broadcast letters each week and follow up with tele-phone calls.

4. Send 50 resumes per month to executive search firms.

5. Telephone ten company executives each week to set up appoint-ments.

6. Answer position-wanted ads in major newspapers.

7. Research companies I would like to work for in my geographical area.

8. Telephone five personal contacts each week.

9. Contact editors of trade journals.
   (a) Review these journals to get a sense of what kinds of positions are being advertised.
   (b) Write ten letters to the editors of the journals I want to contact.
   (c) Check on any seminars or meetings being held in my area that these journals are likely to be interested in.

MY ACTION PLAN

1. _____

    a. _____

    b. _____

    c. _____

    d. _____

2. _____

    a. _____

    b. _____

    c. _____

    d. _____

3. _____

    a. _____

    b. _____

    c. _____

    d. _____

4. _____

    a. _____

    b. _____

    c. _____

    d. _____

5. _____

    a. _____

    b. _____

    c. _____

    d. _____

    _____

    _____

Assigning Priorities and Completion Dates

Now that you've determined the many creative steps you'll be taking to reach your goal, organize these activities in terms of importance. It is vital to also set a time schedule for your overall goal and for the completion of each major step and substep in your action plan. Go back over the personal plan you just designed and add deadline dates. Obviously the completion date for each component must correspond to your target date for the overall plan. In setting these dates, consider the time, money, and energy required.

Although you are establishing priorities, you need not be rigid about staying with your original sequence. Since you will periodically review your progress to ensure that you are moving in the direction you want, you may at some time discover that a shift in priorities is desirable or even essential. At such times, be flexible and adjust your program for success.

Here are some questions to ask yourself periodically, to help you gauge progress in your job search and to keep your action plan in perspective.

- How realistic are my deadline dates?
- What have I learned so far that ought to influence my plan?
- What have I done so far that seems to have the most potential?
- What do I see that might prove to be a roadblock?
- What can I do to get around this potential difficulty?
- What new steps ought I to consider?
- How am I feeling about how things are going?
- What can I do for myself to either maintain or improve this feeling?
- What kinds of follow-up activities should I add to my plan?
- Where can I get more support for my efforts?

You now have an organized approach to finding the right job; the key to success lies in implementing your plans. The important word is *action!* Following through will be a rewarding and highly productive adventure.

Section 4

SELLING YOUR SKILLS AND SIGNING THE CONTRACT

THE INTERVIEW

Just as your resumes, letters, and phone calls serve to introduce and advertise your capabilities and talents to future employers, so the interview is also an essential sales tool.

Getting an interview is the vital beachhead on the way to landing a job. It takes, on the average, about ten interviews to land one job offer. And, ideally, you should have two or three job offers to choose from before you make the big decision. So you're really looking to set up as many as 20 or 30 interviews.

There are five phases to interviewing:

1. Landing the interview.
2. Getting ready for the interview.
3. Handling the interview.
4. Evaluating the interview.
5. Following up the interview.

Landing the Interview

All your efforts so far, including your action plan, have been geared toward getting the interview.

Many of your contacts with future employers require that you be creative and persistent. It is possible that many of your first interviews will be at locations other than the employer's office. You can use your ingenuity in a variety of ways to land the interview when a phone contact is being cut short without the desired appointment being set up.

If the decision maker is giving the impression that he or she is always busy, you may want to say something like:

"I imagine you get to work a lot earlier than the rest of the office. Would it make it easier for you if I came in at 8:00 some morning before the phone starts ringing?"

Or

"Could we have a sandwich together some day next week?"

Or

"I happen to ride the same train you do. Could we share a seat riding home some evening soon?"

With these kinds of individuals, keep trying; many will admire your persistence and unwillingness to take "no" for an answer. Other interviews come more easily, as a result of your advertising efforts. Either way, this is the time to put your best foot forward.

Getting Ready for the Interview

There are two basic types of interviews: screening and in-depth. A screening interview is usually conducted by a personnel interviewer, who will size up your experience and personality, try to uncover your strong and weak points, and compare you with other candidates. The interviewer stands between you and the line manager for whom you will work if hired.

An in-depth interview is usually conducted by a line manager, who will get right down to the business of the interview, to satisfy him- or herself that you do or do not know what you are talking about. The line manager will concentrate on specific dimensions of the job and how you fit them, grasp the points you make as readily as you understand the questions being asked, and look at your expertise, as well as your skills in getting along with people.

Other forms of patterned or structured interviews include psychological, multiple, group, stress, test, social, and telephone.

The objective of the job interview.   The job interview is one of those situations where your goal is clearly to sell yourself. Nothing speaks for you in the interview. You speak for yourself. If there ever is a time to be attentive to the other person, it is in the interview.

The goal of the interview, from the interviewer's point of view, is to determine if your qualifications match the job description. However, even if your qualifications fit the position, the interviewer may not see the facts as you do. Therefore, if you want the job, you must present yourself in a way calculated to convince the interviewer that you offer whatever is needed. The more you are able to convince the interviewer that you do, the greater are your chances that you will be offered the job.

Most interviewers are trained to evaluate data in such a way as to maximize the probability of selecting the correct candidate. The interviewer will be looking for someone who has a certain set of traits, qualities, or abilities that are needed for success on a given job. If the applicant does not seem to possess these qualities, the applicant is eliminated from further consideration.

With these thoughts in mind, it is evident that you need to project yourself in the interview in such a way that the interviewer is made aware of these qualities. In addition, it is critical that you convey your problem-solving skills, job experience, adeptness at relating to others, motivation, and understanding of how to apply your abilities to the position you are interviewing for. Thus, your goal is to create a positive picture in the interviewer's mind so that he or she can translate your experience and skills to the requirements of the job.

In the interview, you will be evaluated on these specific traits:

 1. Analytical ability.
 2. Self-confidence.
 3. Poise.
 4. Decision-making ability.
 5. Aggressiveness.
 6. Job interests.
 7. Past job accomplishments.
 8. Energy level.
 9. Ability to communicate.
10. Stability.
11. Persistence.
12. Maturity.
13. Organizational strengths.
14. Technical knowledge.
15. Job planning expertise.
16. Drive.

17. Ambition.
18. Cooperativeness.

19. Education.
20. Personal achievements.

The 20 traits listed above are categorized into four basic factors:

1. Intellectual skills
    Analytical ability.
    Decision-making ability.
    Expertise in job planning.
    Education.
2. Motivational characteristics
    Job interests.
    Energy level.
    Persistence.
    Drive.
    Ambition.
3. Personality strengths and limita-
    tions

Poise.
Aggressiveness.
Ability to communicate.
Stability.
Maturity.
Cooperativeness.
4. Knowledge and experience
    Self-confidence.
    Goal accomplishments.
    Education.
    Personal achievements.
    Organizational strengths.
    Technical knowledge.

Intellectual Skills. The interviewer, in order to measure your intellectual skills, will be concerned with discovering how well you organize your thoughts and communicate your ideas. Particular attention will be paid to how you think through problems and the logic you use to reach decisions.

Motivational Characteristics. The motivation factor can be evaluated by learning what you like to do or find satisfying. In learning about your motivation, it is helpful for the interviewer to ask you questions about your interests and goals and to evaluate your energy level. Below are some tips on how you can project yourself.

1. Interests. The interviewer will be concerned with your likes and dislikes. To aid you in preparing for this segment of the interview, review the first section of this manual on job likes and dislikes. Also be prepared to speak about specific tasks and responsibilities that you are interested in performing on a job. Elaborating on this question will help the interviewer develop an idea about the kind of work climate that will be most satisfying for you.

2. Ambition. The interviewer will probe you about why you have chosen certain goals or career objectives. Your responses must be well thought out and clearly stated so that the interviewer can relate it to the job description.

3. Energy level. The interviewer will be looking to determine how strong your motivation is to carry you toward the accomplishment of your objectives. A high energy level implies to an interviewer the ability to work diligently without tiring and losing interest as well as to show zest and vitality in your daily work efforts.

Personality strengths and limitations. The interviewer will be concerned with your interpersonal relationships and your skill in coping with people on the job. In attempting to understand your interpersonal skills, the interviewer will evaluate how well you interact with him or her. To a large extent this will depend on "body chemistry." You will likely be judged on the self-confidence, aggressiveness, persuasiveness, forcefulness, and openness you show in the interview itself. The interviewer will also ask you questions to develop a picture of how well you handle such things as coping with stress and gaining cooperation from others.

To evaluate your temperament the interviewer will be concerned with such questions as: Are you rigid? Are you demanding of yourself and/or of others? Are you cautious, sensitive, or impulsive?

Knowledge and experience. Earlier in this manual, we discussed at some length the need for you to identify your job accomplishments and to present your job knowledge and experience in a clear and concise manner. If you are able to relate your work experience in this way, it will enable the interviewer to see how capable you are of learning the skills needed for the job you are seeking, and your chances of success will be greatly increased.

The sequence of the interview. It is common for many interviewers to follow an outline in conducting the interview. To help you prepare, review the following sequence of topics and think through the answers that are necessary for you to present yourself in an intelligent manner.

> Early family life.
> High school and/or college achievements.
> Military experience.
> Summer and full- or part-time work experience.
> Attitudes toward job and employees.
> Goals and career objectives.
> Self-assessment of your strengths and weaknesses.
> Personal background.
> Leisure activities and hobbies.

Handling the Interview

When you are called in for your first interview, you should realize that this is a get-acquainted meeting. It may be conducted by someone from personnel or with a cadre of interviewers. This gives you an opportunity to present your wares. It is a crucial situation and will not generally be repeated if you fail to present yourself in a professional manner. So make up your mind at the outset when you step through the door that you are a winner. If you want to win, act like it. Walk into the interviewer's office erect, shake hands firmly, smile, and above all, relax.

You must control the interview by using your own outline, shown below.

1. *Who am I?* Give a brief overview of your professional life. Make your presentation a capsulized account that runs no longer than two to three minutes.

2. *Who are you?* Here's your opportunity to get details and general information about the company and the position in question. Be sure to ask questions and practice good listening techniques.

3. *State accomplishments.* Memorize four to six of your accomplishments and be prepared to feed these to the interviewer so that he or she can easily understand how your job duties and past accomplishments meet the requirements of the position. Establish a needs–benefit linkup.

4. *Summarize.* At the conclusion of the interview, be sure to summarize your experience in a manner that relates to the job opening. In addition, be sure that you know what the next step in the process is and whether you will be asked to move into the second interview proceedings. If you think that the interviewer is stalling or hesitant to tell you where you stand, push for the reason. It may be that the interviewer still isn't sure how you will fit into the position. If this situation is evident, attempt to restate your accomplishments.

Asking and answering questions. The following is a list of some of the questions that you should ask during the early stages of an interview.

1. In what way has the position been handled in the past?
2. What are the current responsibilities of the position?
3. Can this position offer me the growth that I am seeking?
4. What part does this job play in the overall objectives of the organization?
5. Is the job sharply defined, or can it be expanded and changed as the organization grows?
6. What is the commitment of the company to this job?
7. What has happened to the individual who held this position before?
8. What can I expect in career growth if I meet the expectations of the job?

Don't be afraid to raise these questions. The potential employer will respect your concern.

Reply to all the interviewer's questions in a positive and specific manner. Don't let the conversation wander from the issue at hand—a better job. Dramatize this effectively by utilizing samples of related and proven experience.

Below are some tips for dealing with difficult questions an interviewer might ask:

1. What do you know about our company?
   ○ Be prepared with some information about such things as products, size, income, reputation, image, goals, problems, management talent, management style, people, skills, history, and philosophy.

    ○ Don't say you don't know much; state that you would like to know more.

2. Why do you want to work for us?
   ○ Mention a company project you would like to be part of or a company problem you think you can help solve.
   ○ Describe some contribution you think you can make to specific company goals.

3. What can you do for us that someone else can't?
   ○ Relate past success in solving previous employer problem(s) that may be similar to those of the prospective employer.

4. What do you find most attractive about our position?
   ○ Mention the challenge of the assignment and the opportunity to achieve results.

5. Why should we hire you?
   ○ Cite a need you can fill. Refer to your relevant skills.

6. What do you look for in a job?
   ○ Include opportunities to use your specific capabilities and to increase and develop your skills.

7. Please give me your definition of a _____ (the position for which you are being interviewed).

8. How long would it take you to make a meaningful contribution to our firm?
   ○ Don't undersell or oversell yourself. If you can convert immediate task responsibility into meaningful contributions, do so. For example, "It may take some months before I can . . . , but. . . ."

9. How long would you stay with us?
   ○ Meaningful answers do not have to include time periods of months and years. For example, you might reply "As long as . . . ."

10. Don't you feel a little old/young for this job?
    ○ Move from age to capabilities. For example, "My past experience indicates to me that I perform best in the type of job you have described."

11. You may be overqualified or too experienced for the position we have to offer.
    ○ Possible answers include: "A strong company needs a strong person"; "Experienced executives are at a premium today"; "A growing, energetic company rarely is unable to use the talents of its employees."
    ○ Emphasize interest in long-term association.
    ○ Say that the employer will get a faster return on investment because you have more experience than required.

12. What is your philosophy of management?
    ○ If you've never thought about this, it's high time you did so.

13. What is your management style?

- ○ Refer to your abilities to set goals, objectives, and action plans and mention that you encourage participative management by getting input from your staff.

14. Are you a good _____?
    - ○ Give examples.
15. As a manager, what did you look for when you hired people?
    - ○ Refer to skills, initiative, adaptability.
16. As a manager, did you ever fire anyone? If so, what were the reasons and how did you handle it?
17. What do you see as the most difficult task in being a manager or an executive?
    - ○ A good answer might be: "Getting things planned and done."
18. What important trends do you see in our industry?
    - ○ If you're a novice in the industry, don't fake it.
19. What are the "frontier" issues of your profession?
    - ○ Be direct; don't "soapbox."
20. Why are you leaving your present job?
    - ○ Give a nonpersonal answer when possible. For example, "Our office is closing."
    - ○ Stick to one response; don't change answers during the interview.
21. How do you feel about leaving all of your benefits?
22. Describe what you feel to be an ideal working environment.
23. How would you evaluate the firm you are currently working for?
    - ○ Be balanced. State both negatives and positives.
24. Have you helped increase sales? Profits? How?
25. Have you helped reduce costs? How?
26. How much money did you ever account for?
27. How many people did you supervise on your last job?
28. Do you like working with figures more than with words?
29. What do your subordinates think of you?
30. In your current or last position, what features did you like the most? Least?
31. What are your five most significant accomplishments in your current or last position? In your career so far?
    - ○ Memorize these.
32. Why haven't you found a new position before now?
    - ○ Don't apologize. Don't defend.
33. Had you thought of leaving your present position before? If yes, what do you think held you there?
34. What do you think of your boss?
35. Would you describe a few situations in which your work was criticized?
    - ○ Demonstrate how you turn criticism into an opportunity to learn and improve.

36. If I spoke with your previous boss, what would he or she say are your greatest strengths and weaknesses?
37. Can you work under pressure?
38. How have you changed the nature of your job?
39. Do you prefer staff or line work? Why?
40. In your present position, what problems have you identified that had previously been overlooked?
41. Don't you feel you might be better off in a different size company? Different type company?
42. If you had your choice of jobs and companies, where would you go?
43. Why aren't you earning more at your age?
    ○ You might say that salary has been only one of several important considerations.
44. What do you think this position should pay?
    ○ Answer with a question. That is, "What is the salary range for similar jobs in your company?"
45. What salary do you expect if we offer this position to you?
    ○ Be careful; the market value of the job may be the key answer. For example, "My understanding is that a job like the one you're describing may be in the range of $_____."
46. What kind of salary are you worth?
    ○ You'd better be worth at least what the job pays.
47. Any objections to psychological tests?
    ○ There's no use debating this. If you're willing to take the tests, why red-flag your reservations?
48. Tell me about yourself.
    ○ Be on guard against the interviewer who gives you free rein.
    ○ Don't spend much time answering (1½–2 minutes); avoid detail; don't ramble.
    ○ Relate your answer to the job opening.
    ○ State what you can do for the employer.
    ○ Turn it back with "What else would you like to know about me?"
49. What other types of jobs and companies are you considering?
50. Do you generally speak to people before they speak to you?
51. What was the last book you read? Movie you saw? Sporting event you attended?
52. Will you be out to take your boss's job?
53. Are you creative?
    ○ Give examples.
54. How would you describe your own personality?
    ○ Be balanced, but essentially focus on the positive.
55. Are you a leader?
    ○ Give examples.

   ○ Point out that most positions require both the ability to lead (take initiative, set a model) and to follow (respond to needs and directives).

56. What are your goals?
    ○ Avoid statements such as "I would like the job you advertised." Instead, give long-range goals.
    ○ Relate your answer to the employer rather than giving a self-serving reply—"In a firm such as yours, I would like to be . . . ." not "I am so capable I should be . . . ."

57. What are your strong points?
    ○ Present at least three.
    ○ Relate them to the interviewing company and job opening.

58. What are your weak points?
    ○ Don't say you have none.
    ○ Turn a negative into a positive answer. For example, "I am sometimes impatient and do the work myself when we are late."

59. Why didn't you do better in college?

60. How do you feel about people from minority groups?
    ○ If you're not prejudiced, show it by not lumping people together. A good answer might be "I see people as individuals."

61. Would you object to working for a woman?

62. What position do you expect to have in five years?
    ○ Respond in terms of objectives (responsibilities, accomplishments) rather than job titles. For example, "A job in which I can . . . ."

63. What are you doing, or what have you done, to reach those objectives?
    ○ Give yourself credit.

64. If you could start again, what would you do differently?

65. What career options do you have at the moment?

66. How would you describe the essence of success? According to your definition of success, how successful have you been so far?
    ○ If your personal opinion is that you've not been successful per your definition, talk about the success of being able to know when a new direction is needed and having the initiative and courage to take it.

You need to project the right image for your future employer, and that begins even before you two begin talking. So, again remember these key points:

○ Be on time. Don't smoke. Consider the secretary as your first interviewer. Be your best self even with him or her.
○ Leave your briefcase and other paperwork home. Have a resume in your inside pocket or handbag in case the interviewer insists on having one or you think it desirable to leave it after the interview is completed.
○ Remember that how you look, how you sound, the sense you convey of how you feel will all make an impact on your interviewer. So walk into his or her office seeing yourself as someone with talents and abilities and tell

yourself that you have something valuable to contribute, so you can feel confident about yourself and your ability to perform. This doesn't mean cockiness, of course, but rather sureness. (The interviewer is probably also concerned about his or her ability to express views articulately. You have been contacted because the interviewer has deduced that you may have something valuable to offer. You need only to verify it.)

○ Be sure your voice is loud enough to make it easy to hear and to convey a sense of energy and strength.

○ Be sure you know what the interviewer is asking. Paraphrase what you heard to check out your understanding of the question.

○ If you cannot answer the question, acknowledge that without long-winded explanations or apologies.

○ Stick to the point in your responses. Speak concisely and briefly. Don't ramble. Use "I" language. Stop when you've answered the question.

○ Avoid using your key material in response to the first couple of questions. It takes a while for your interviewer to fully concentrate on you and your accomplishments, so don't waste any of your most powerful data before you have established rapport.

○ Use your eyes and ears to get a sense of your interviewer's style, language, mannerisms, and surroundings, and, to the extent you can do so comfortably, match him or her in formality or informality, language style, even choice of words.

○ Strive for a natural dialogue with the interviewer. Ask as well as answer. Invite the interviewer to talk and initiate an exchange of ideas by asking strategic questions about the job, the company, its objectives—questions that show you've done some homework on the company. Express your interest in the company and its future as well as how you might be a part of that future.

○ Be positive. Deliberately choose positive words to replace negative ones. For example, use "challenge" rather than "problem," "opportunity to learn and change" rather than "mistake."

○ Be active in your attempts to discover all you can about the potential job and its specific responsibilities. Relate what you hear to your past experience and accomplishments. Connect the company's needs with your ability to meet those needs. But if the job and you are really not a match, acknowledge it both to yourself and to the interviewer.

○ Even if you feel the interviewer is wrong, do not criticize. You never know what people he or she knows who could be of help to you in future interviews.

○ Avoid discussing such potentially volatile subjects as religion, politics, and previous employers' personalities.

○ Be truthful; don't oversell or undersell yourself. Your accomplishments are what you are selling. Let the interviewer sell you on the company.

- Some interviewers will deliberately try to create stress situations to test how you react under pressure. Don't fall for this game; use common sense in handling yourself. Terminate the interview if it becomes unproductive. Don't argue; change the flow of the interview if you feel your temperature rising. You can do this by asking a nonthreatening question.
- Strive to delay all mention of money until the end of the interview. If your minimum requirement is sought early, parry with the need to learn more about the scope of the job, since the service you can provide, not income, is the principal question. If the interviewer insists, you can at least tell what you have been earning and indicate you would hope to progress.
- Avoid naming your references or allowing them to be contacted until you and the prospective employer have come to some agreement—that is, arranged for a second interview or discussed a job offer.
- Always determine the next step in your dealings before leaving the interviewer's office. If no second interview is definitely set, restate your qualifications to fill the position and ask when the interviewer expects to make some preliminary evaluation and if it would be convenient for you to contact him or her.

All of the above are meant as guidelines for you in conducting a successful interview. Do not push yourself to memorize them or allow yourself to be so bound by these helpful hints that you become rigid and appear stilted. All in all, what you want to be is AT EASE:

Ask if you didn't hear or understand the question thoroughly. Ask questions about the job, its objectives, and the future of the position.

Tell the interviewer when you can't answer a question. Be assertive.

Employ positive and specific descriptions about yourself, and above all, stress your accomplishments.

Answer all questions in a concise manner, without rambling or hesitating.

Seize opportunities to get in your "good licks" about how you could help your new employer, by discussing your skills and abilities.

End when you've answered the question. Summarize the interview to be sure you have stated your experience in a logical manner.

Evaluating the Interview

After each job interview, use the following questions to evaluate how well you performed. Build up your self-observation skills by responding to these questions yourself.

1. Do you feel good about how it went?
2. What did you do or say that particularly pleases you?
3. What did you do or say that you think needs improvement?

4. Did you listen, without interrupting, to what the company or boss needed?
5. What questions were asked that you think you need more practice in answering?
6. Did you articulate your relevant talents, skills, and experience?
7. Did you make an opportunity to communicate your accomplishments?
8. Did you, by words and manner, create a positive picture?
9. Did you stick to relevant issues without rambling?
10. Was your voice firm and strong?
11. What phase of the interview was easiest for you?
12. What phase of the interview was hardest for you?
13. What, if any, additional training do you want from your counselor?
14. Were you *at ease?*
15. Is the job described one you would be interested in securing?
16. Did you leave with an atmosphere of mutual respect and regard?
17. Did the interviewer like you? How do you know?
18. Is there a plan for you to come back?
19. What follow-up steps would be appropriate?

Following Up the Interview

After an interview, prepare a follow-up letter to the manager with whom you spoke:

1. Thank the manager for the interview.
2. Emphasize your interest for the position in question.
3. Rephrase your background and briefly explain how your experience can complement the requirements of the position.
4. Indicate that you intend to follow up the letter with a telephone call to determine if and when the interviewer wishes to see you again.

Take a look at Figure 30. If the position you interviewed for is not a job you desire, you should still send a follow-up letter expressing your thanks and informing the interviewer of your decision. If you are still interested in the company and would like to be considered for other positions that are more in line with your background and interests, then let the company know this.

FIGURE 30. Sample interview follow-up letter.

Mr. A. L. Benson, President
Microwaves Unlimited
317 Hillcrest Avenue
Stamford, Connecticut 06906

Dear Mr. Benson:

Having just gotten back from my trip East, I wanted to thank you for a pleasant lunch session early this week—and also offer you some further ideas that came to me after our meeting.

First, let me say that I understand fully that your entry into the consumer market is still "on the drawing boards." As a matter of fact, this is one of the aspects of your company that is most interesting to me—the opportunity to get into a new business venture on the ground floor and see it really grow.

In thinking about this new venture, the idea that occurred to me—and no doubt it has to you also—is the eventual synergism that you could attain in consumer marketing of microwave equipment through the excellent reputation and broad consciousness you have already established in your successful marketing of CB radio equipment.

I feel that my own experience in sophisticated electronics for the retail trade, although by no means identical with your product line, gives me a fair amount of know-how that would be rather quickly applicable in your new business.

At any rate, the forward thinking that you described was most exciting for me, and I do hope that we will get a chance to explore it further together.

In the meantime, I have attached an updated resume that gives a bit more specific information about some of my undertakings and accomplishments with my present employer. Hope these will be relevant and useful for you. I will call you in a few days so that we can further explore some ideas.

Again, many thanks.

Yours very truly,

Robert F. Jackson

DETERMINING WHERE YOU STAND

It is good to know where you stand with the companies you have interviewed with, so that you can be fully prepared when you are called on to enter into serious and final negotiations or to make a decision. You need to be able to balance your negotiations with all interested companies in a way that is best for you.

There are a number of clues that reveal how seriously interested in you a company is. For example, any time you get past the first screening interview and are invited to meet other people, that is a strong signal. It is especially strong when you are invited to meet the line manager or decision maker. Signals get louder when he or she spends a great deal more time with you than originally scheduled for your interview.

Naturally, if the company invites you to visit some of its locations that would be under your jurisdiction, or asks you to visit its consultant or psychologist, you are getting still closer. Being asked to give references or take tests are two other loud signals.

If an executive search firm sends you or takes you to meet its client, this usually means that you are one of the small handful that are being tested out as probable candidates.

And finally, if you have some uncertainty about where you stand, a very simple way to find out is merely to ask. Then it is likely that the company will tell you if it has narrowed down the field to a few candidates and if you are a strong competitor.

Getting a job and filling a job opening are reciprocal exercises. You are weighing one company against another, one job against another, one staff against another, one location against another, one workload against another. The company is weighing one candidate against another. Sometimes, even, a company is weighing whether or not to actually hire anyone new. Each of you is sensibly looking out for your own best interests. To protect *your* best interests:

1. Follow up with companies as per their request, but don't follow up too frequently or appear too anxious. It puts you in a position of weakness.
2. Don't divulge the details of your negotiations with various companies with anyone. Don't mention company names, dollar levels, people you are dealing with, how many interviews you've had, etc.
3. Don't be lulled into inactivity prematurely because you are picking up signals that a company is seriously interested in hiring you. Until you receive an official confirmation of a job offer, keep going with your full program of job-hunting activities; don't let other leads go stale. Here are

some reasons why a seemingly sure thing sometimes doesn't materialize:

- A better candidate shows up at the last minute.
- The board fails to approve either the position or the salary.
- The parent company sends out an instant freeze on all hiring.
- A sudden merger or takeover threat paralyzes the management.
- The person you were talking to turns out not to be the decision maker, or he or she didn't have the final authority to hire.
- The decision maker merely wanted to show the boss that there are better people out there than "old Charlie."
- Questions arose during the reference-checking process.
- You yourself did something to blow it in the final stages.
- The company decided that an insider from its own ranks could do the job after all.
- Somebody up there didn't allow money in the budget.

4. Think through carefully each move you make. If you get into a situation that puzzles you, do not make a quick commitment or abruptly discontinue efforts. Ask for time to think it over and then discuss the problem with a reliable friend.

GETTING THE BEST DEAL

In the early stages of exploration, the burden was upon you to demonstrate your ability to respond to the company's needs. Now you must declare your own needs.

A way to lead into this discussion is to summarize or recap what you feel are the needs of the company, the boss, and the job and how you can fill these needs excellently. Then it's time to say something like: "I've also been thinking about some of my own needs and those of my family, and I wonder if we could now get to these topics."

Salary

If there is a gap between the salary they are suggesting and what you really would like, you may be able to advance such reasoning as:

- You need to feel that you are truly advancing over your current position. A customary step up, assuming living costs are comparable, is a 10–20 percent increase. It needs to be higher in the higher salary levels, because taxes take a bigger bite.
- You still have three children to put through college, which will be a heavy expense for several years.
- Moving to the big city will bring not only an increase in living expenses but also higher state and city taxes.

Some decision makers like to drive a hard bargain, when in truth they have leeway to pay more if they like you. Your tactic is to express your needs and, without breaking off discussion prematurely, feel out how much latitude there is in their position.

Company Benefits

Larger companies tend to have a fairly complete package of benefits—health insurance, life insurance, accidental death and disability insurance, travel insurance, survivor income, pensions—that may be presented to you as company policy and not subject to negotiation. However, if a company wants you badly enough, and particularly if you are at the executive level, some of these things are negotiable. For example, if you have moved around the corporate world without acquiring much pension for your older age, it may be entirely possible for you to negotiate a special pension plan that makes up a good part of your need.

Additional Income

One of the common routes to get more pay than just a base salary is through a bonus plan, based on either true performance (individual or through a group) or a routine add-on. Then there are all sorts of performance plans, profit sharing plans, stock options (qualified and nonqualified), deferred income plans, and many other sources of additional income. Often your eligibility to join one of these plans is negotiable, and how soon you can be admitted is likewise open to bargaining. If you think the rest of the package that you are negotiating is a little on the skimpy side, additional income can improve the bargain. If you happen to be in a high tax bracket, these special forms of compensation take on extra importance.

Perquisites

Many perquisites, such as a company car, club membership, a corner office, a private secretary, and even job title and scope, are negotiable.

Relocation Expenses

Some companies have general policies allowing for moving expenses, house hunting, and the general cost of relocating; these too may be subject to individual negotiation.

As you get into the swing of the final negotiations, you must differentiate between those things that you are flexible about and those that you consider nonnegotiable. Differentiate also between making statements and making demands. Top executives, if they feel challenged or think you are trying to take control, may react by showing their power and knocking you out of the running. One way to avoid this sort of contest is to explain what you need or would like and check out how the decision maker and the company respond. Find out how your requirements fit into the company's scheme of contracting with employees. Often, what a company will negotiate with you is measured, not so much by what they think you are worth, but by the contracting models they are already using with other employees at a similar level.

When you have reached as good a bargain as you apparently can, ask for a day or so to study it before you commit yourself. You may even need considerably longer, depending on the stage you're at with other companies. During this examination time, make careful calculations to check whether the whole proposition would end up being tolerable, a real gain, or a serious loss. Among the items that sometimes surprise job changers are higher living costs—high cost of housing and land; higher state, city, and real estate taxes; commuter costs; etc. Build in an opportunity for you to consider these realities before making a firm contract.

KEEPING YOUR OPTIONS OPEN

It is both a pleasant and an agonizing experience to have more than one job offer, either in hand or apparently close. Of course, if the company you most favor has made a firm, attractive offer, your decision-making process is simplified.

If, however, the company (No. 1) you favor has not made a firm offer, while another company (No. 2) is pressing hard for a decision on its offer, which you consider a viable option, you must act in your own behalf to keep your options open. Don't make a decision on the offer in hand without knowing what may be just around the corner for you.

You and Company No. 1

Lean gently on the laggard company. Say something like: "In order to deal forthrightly with the other company, I feel obliged to give them an answer on their fine offer. But I would really prefer to hear something from you folks and am hoping it would be attractive too."

There are many reasons why companies may be sincerely interested in a candidate but don't quite get around to finalizing an offer. Often hiring at the middle to upper level requires a group of people—the salary committee, the board, the executive committee—to meet and approve the decision. Perhaps one of the key people is out of the city. Or there may truly have been pressing business matters that made it impossible to get together and consider your candidacy.

On the other hand, if your favorite company seems truly to be dragging its feet, it is perfectly proper for you to ask your contact for a frank appraisal of where you stand. Do they have other candidates they need to see? Are there other people that need to be brought into the decision? How long a delay do they anticipate?

Sometimes a dramatic move will get it off dead center. For example, you could offer to jump on a plane and fly down to meet the key person for dinner, so that you both could get a still better sense of how you could work together.

You and Company No. 2

Test out their willingness to wait with a request along these lines: "I have another job possibility that is in a very similar stage, and I wonder if you can comfortably give me ten days or so to survey my whole situation and thus make a careful decision." If they don't want to give you ten days, they may offer you a shorter term, or happily, they may say, "Take all the time you need." It is important to explore their feelings, however, since the hiring romance can cool instantly if a company thinks that you are playing games.

If you decide to accept the job from a company you have worked with extensively, be sure to sign off on a pleasant note. If the lack of agreement is over some condition of employment, such as salary, it is not uncommon for a company to come back several months later and up the ante. Or it could happen that two years from now, the company will remember you favorably when a still bigger job comes up.

If a company you have held high interest in decides not to offer you a position, you might consider writing a letter of acknowledgment (see Figure 31 for a sample) that may elicit feedback to facilitate the rest of your job search and, at the same time, will keep the door open for future contact.

FIGURE 31. Sample letter of acknowledgment of job not offered.

Dear Mrs. Frank:

I found it a profitable experience to explore the potential of my joining you at HRI as an organizational consultant. As we discussed the needs of your agency, I found myself making notes of new approaches to help personnel in human service agencies function at peak performance without wearing themselves out. I'll be developing these new directions in future seminar designs.

I enjoyed our conversations together and appreciated the mutual respect and peership that developed. I also appreciated the extended time that Dr. Hathaway gave to our explorations.

Thank you for letting me know so promptly your decision not to invite me at the present time to join HRI. I am sure that your decision was made thoughtfully. I would be pleased to know what aspects of my background or presentation contributed to that decision. Your response would constitute valuable feedback for which I would be very appreciative.

I look forward to hearing from you. I wish you and your staff continued success in the fine services you offer the community.

Sincerely,

Robert Erving

MAKING THE FINAL DECISION

The task of finding a job can be wearing, both physically and psychologically, and you may be vulnerable to jumping at something just because you are sick and tired of continuing the effort.

If the job you are offered rates high and you anticipate a really positive future in it, you are ready to make a decision and are probably feeling excited about that. But if you experience much hesitation about making a real commitment to any of the offers, take a fresh look at what you postulated as your goals when you designed your action plan. Ask yourself:

- Would it be better to reject all the current offers?
- Should I modify my original parameters and specifications?
- Have I really used up all my good leads at the moment?
- If so, is it possible to develop more? Or am I seeking my job in a rather limited field?
- How long would it take to rekindle new fires and find new job leads?
- Where do I stand with regard to my termination arrangements and financial staying power?
- Have I been out of work so long that it seems prudent to just take any job?

CONFIRMING THE DECISION

When you receive a verbal offer, find out if there are any further conditions preliminary to your employment, such as a medical examination or further checking. Review orally your understanding of the agreement, and see if your future boss concurs.

Then ask your new boss if he or she would feel comfortable giving you a confirming letter before you cut loose your present job or other job leads. In case the company is not experienced in confirming offers this way, you might explain that what you want is a statement that you are offered a certain job with a certain title, salary, and other negotiated benefits. Also, the starting date should be spelled out. In some cases, it is a good idea to mention the person to whom you will be reporting and which functions or departments will be reporting to you.

Or you may offer to write a letter of acceptance in duplicate, including all the above details, and have your new boss sign and return one copy as confirmation.

You may wonder why the letter of confirmation is important. It is true that not one in a hundred companies will welsh on an offer. But it does happen. One of our clients received an offer and was told to go ahead and sell his home and proceed to move. He did exactly this, then received word that the board of directors had declined to approve filling the job. Possibly he might have sued, but that wouldn't have helped him in his main goal—to get a new job.

If a company refuses to put their offer in writing, it may be a cautionary signal.

Section 5

PLANNING YOUR STRATEGIES FOR UPWARD MOBILITY

You've worked hard, you've worked long, and you've reaped the rewards: the job you sought. it's time to congratulate yourself and begin the next task—to set in motion an ongoing evaluation system that will help you get off on the right foot, keep you tuned in to how you're doing and feeling on this job, and alert you to that moment in the future when it's time to move on.

STARTING ON THE RIGHT FOOT

Come to your new position with an open mind—one that takes the attitude that you're there both to do and to learn. There is a fine line to tread between adapting to your new organization and its norms and styles and being creative and innovative. So arrive at your new office with eyes and ears open. Suspend judgment as you seek to discover the actual functioning of this company. You're going to be watching and listening to identify the existing networks in your organization.

Power networks. The real power and authority networks are not always those listed in the organizational manual or those delineated in the written hierarchical structure. Who really reports to whom? Who makes the decisions about expenditures? Who makes the decisions about new directions? Who makes the decisions about implementation? Whose criticism is most attended to? Whose advice is sought after? Whose decision can be countermanded—and by whom? Whose suggestions are treated like orders? Whose opinion, when voiced, leads others to modify and alter their own opinions? Who acts without waiting for approval—and is rewarded for doing it? Who is habitually turned to as spokesperson? At whom do personnel glance as they air their views, their recommendations?

Communications networks. Who speaks to whom? Who confides in whom? What is the chain of individuals it's necessary to go through to reach a decision maker? Who serves as intermediary between others? Who lunches together?

Support networks: What are the social alliances? Who regularly backs up whose ideas? Who pitches in with real-hour work to help another? Who seems to be locked in a personality clash with whom?

Now that you've identified the existing power, communications, and support networks, you are in a better position to fit into the existing systems when appropriate and to create new personal networks for your own comfort and advancement. To do this effectively, however, you must set up feedback networks on the job to discover how you are seen in terms of your productive functioning and your ability to form positive relationships.

BUILDING FEEDBACK NETWORKS

The feedback you want will come from three sources: your subordinates, your colleagues, and your supervisor. It will come in a variety of forms, such as how and how often you are approached, whether your opinion is sought after, the tone of voice with which people talk to you, the feel of warmth or coolness with which you are contacted, the unspoken messages you notice, the commendations and criticisms that are offered, and the frequency and kind of outreach that others make toward you. Remember that all behavior is in some measure feedback. If you are not getting the responses you want from others, it is an indication to alter your behavior. You do not, however, need to be passive in getting this feedback, nor do you need to leave the bulk of the feedback you receive open to interpretation. You can take an active part in eliciting this feedback.

One way to go after feedback directly is to ask for it. Following are some suggestions for the kinds of questions that will help you elicit the professional and personal feedback that you can then use to make any necessary changes in your behavior.

With your subordinates:
- Do you understand my expectations of you?
- How could I communicate more clearly to you?
- Are you getting as much supervision as you need and are comfortable with? Are you getting too much?
- How could I be more helpful to you in the performance of your job?
- Are you getting the support you want? What's missing for you?
- Are you getting enough specific, detailed feedback so that you know where you stand with me?
- Are you feeling pushed beyond your limits? Not used enough?
- Are you getting balanced feedback, that is, both positive and negative?
- Do you feel comfortable in coming to me when you're stuck? If not, what gets in the way?
- What could I do to help you function more effectively and efficiently?

With your colleagues:
- Are you comfortable that we don't get in each other's way? If not, how do we become comfortable with each other?
- Are you getting the support you want from me? What's missing for you?
- How can we make each other's job easier? More effective?
- What do you notice has changed since I joined the staff?

With your supervisor:
- What's your overall comment on the progress I'm making?
- How is my performance fitting in with your expectations of me?
- Are there areas in which you wish I were taking more initiative? Less initiative?
- How could I communicate more clearly to you?
- Are you comfortable with the amount of reporting I do to you? If not, what specifically would you like?
- How specifically do you see my relationships with my colleagues and subordinates? Are there any changes you would recommend?

○ How are you feeling about our work together? Are there any changes you would recommend?

These questions can be asked directly, or they can be approached via a more general talk about "how things are going." One of the advantages about the direct question is that, in asking it, you are also communicating directly to another that you have a desire to know what he or she is thinking and are open to hearing it. In this way, you set up a channel and a model for feedback that, in the future, will encourage others to offer you constructive criticism even if you aren't aware that it's time to ask for it. Thus, trouble can be nipped in the bud; you will have established with subordinates, peers, and bosses a medium of communication that will serve to keep you abreast of how you are being viewed, personally and professionally.

SELF-EVALUATION

How you rate your role and your productivity and how you are feeling at the job is just as important as how others see you. Set aside time after two months, then six months, on the job to do a thorough assessment of how things are going. In addition, use the following evaluation on a regular basis.

How Do I Feel?

Listed below are potential complaints. Check each statement that applies to you in your present job.

___ You don't make enough money to meet your needs.

___ You are paid poorly relative to other people.

___ Fringe benefits are inadequate.

___ Your job is overtaxing physically and/or mentally.

___ Your physical environment is unhealthy or unpleasant.

___ You are bored.

___ You don't have a clear understanding of the goals of the company.

___ You are at odds with the goals of the company.

___ You think you are taken for granted at work.

___ You think you ought to be doing something more important.

___ Your job interferes with other aspects of your life.

___ Your good work is not rewarded.

— You don't have access to your boss.

— You are subjected to discrimination.

— You drag yourself to work each day.

— There isn't anyone to talk to about dissatisfactions.

— You don't feel support from your boss or colleagues.

— The work you're doing isn't what you anticipated when you started the job.

— You can't seem to get along with key people.

— You feel overworked.

— Underworked.

— You leave your job each day feeling exhausted.

— You frequently catch yourself daydreaming.

— Off the job, you frequently lose your temper or sulk because of work tensions.

— You feel you are oversupervised.

— You feel you are undersupervised.

— Your morale is bad.

— There is an air of secrecy concerning company policies.

— Because of your job, you experience unexplained physical or mental discomforts or pain.

— You think your job is causing you to become dependent upon alcohol, tranquilizers, or other pills.

To further highlight your feelings on and about the job, read the adjectives listed below and check each that applies to you.

— Abused	— Coerced	— Envious
— Angry	— Confident	— Esteemed
— Antagonistic	— Creative	— Excluded
— Anxious	— Cynical	— Fragmented
— Appreciated	— Defensive	— Frustrated
— Bored	— Despairing	— Fulfilled
— Challenged	— Desperate	— Growing
— Cheap	— Distrusting	— Happy

__ Hurt	__ Rewarded	__ Trapped
__ Ignored	__ Frightened	__ Trusted
__ Intimidated	__ Satisfied	__ Undecided
__ Lost	__ Secure	__ Used
__ Overlooked	__ Sick	__ Persecuted
__ Pressured	__ Stunted	__ Valued
__ Proud	__ Stymied	__ Weary
__ Respected	__ Threatened	

How Am I Doing?

In this realm, too, your self-questioning should cover your behavior on an interpersonal as well as a professional level. Can you answer "yes" to most of the following questions?

- Do I carry my share of responsibility?
- Do I delegate authority when it's appropriate?
- Am I able to diagnose the problems that arise?
- Am I creative in generating solutions?
- Am I tactful and diplomatic with others?
- Do I offer honest praise to others?
- Am I adding frequently to my ongoing list of accomplishments?
- Is my thinking free of stereotyped patterns?
- Do I probe deeply to get and evaluate information?
- Am I thorough enough in my work?
- Do I effectively pass on information that those around and above me need in order to act intelligently?
- Do I get my associates to tell me what their needs are?
- Am I flexible in adjusting to the demands of people and situations?
- Am I a good listener?
- Do I get my job done without needing to be pushed?
- Do I keep my cool under stress?
- Do people tend to come to me for advice?
- Do I generally deliver what I promise to others?
- Am I generally accurate at predicting the behavior of others?
- Am I effective in keeping my feelings from getting mixed up in using good judgment?
- Do I uses my general knowledge and my knowledge of others to good advantage?
- Do I tend to work "smart" rather than hard?
- Am I easily intimidated by my managers?

Where Do I Stand?

These questions are meant to orient you to your professional growth and your current place in your organization, which together will further or impede your full career development. Can you answer "yes" to most of them?

○ Are you being included in the communications network?
○ Is your job worth preserving, even in a budget crunch?
○ Are you and your accomplishments visible to those in the power network?
○ Are you maintaining an ongoing record of your accomplishments?
○ Are you growing in your capacity to handle your present. and future responsibilities?
○ Are you keeping up with new developments in your field?
○ Do you have easy access to those decision makers who have the authority to promote you?
○ Have you arranged for periodic feedback sessions with your boss?
○ Are your present responsibilities in keeping with your long-range career objectives?
○ Are you maintaining connections with your personal contact network?
○ Are you in a department or company that has room for you to grow?
○ Do you know what the organizational standard for "outstanding performer" is?

TROUBLESHOOTING

It is likely that at some point you will get some feedback either from others or from yourself that indicates that it's time to do some remedial work.

The first question to ask yourself is: "Who or what needs to change?" That is, does the change need to be made in yourself, in some others(s), or in some aspect of the environment. For example, suppose that you had responded "yes" to the issue of feeling overworked. The remedy for that fatiguing and stressful condition may lie in your own behavior or attitude, in the behavior of your supervisor or colleagues, or in the nature of conditions of your job itself.

To help you understand the situation better, ask yourself:

○ Are you organizing your time poorly, so that you're frequently faced with rush jobs?
○ Are you taking on other people's responsibilities when you would do better to say "no" to them?
○ Are you in over your head so that each job requires more energy from you than it would if you were working at your best level of competence?

Or

○ Is your boss continually loading assignments on you without regard for your present workload?

○ Are subordinates slipping behind, putting you into the position of having to take over for them to complete those aspects of the job for which you are accountable?

○ Are some colleagues eating up your time in casual talk, leaving you feeling way behind at the end of the day?

Or

○ Is the office understaffed?

○ Have the departmental hiring procedures not kept up with the departmental responsibilities?

○ Are the materials you need to do your work in an unaccessible place, putting additional and unnecessary time pressures on you?

Until you've diagnosed the source of the problem, you will be handicapped in effecting an efficient and easy solution. So, in troubleshooting, both to reduce stress on yourself and to facilitate the necessary change, find out where that change needs to occur.

RESPONDING TO TROUBLE

Trouble on the job—whether physical, emotional, interpersonal, or professional—causes stress. Stress is sometimes a motivator for increased output and productivity. It is also, particularly when it is excessive or when your ability to deal with it is limited, a cause of impaired efficiency and difficult relationships. Both of these reduce your capacity for full progress toward your career objective.

What are your choices when you find yourself in conflict on the job? You can:

1. Stick to your guns (just keep doing the job the best you can; if you complain, do it ineffectively; just keep going and hope something good will happen).

2. Get out of the situation (quit your job; ask for a transfer; ask for a new office).

3. Change the situational demand (get your job description rewritten; get more funds allocated for additional staff; convince your boss, colleagues, subordinates to change; get the other person fired or transferred; lobby for better working conditions).

4. Change your behavior (work harder—or less hard; learn to say "no" to added work demands—or to say "yes"; speak up more at meetings—or

practice listening while others have their say; get your own coffee—or get others theirs).

5. Change your attitude (welcome challenges instead of dreading problems; consider a competitor at work as a reason to stay on your toes; be flattered by your supervisor's close attention to you, viewing it as an opportunity to demonstrate your talents).

6. Pretend that you've altered your perception of the problem (tell your boss you're flattered by his or her close supervision and seethe inside; assure new members of the staff that you welcome their participation and spend energy trying to figure out how to show them up).

Of these choices, No. 1, to tough it out, and No. 6, to mask it and pretend it isn't there, take no effective action to deal with or resolve the conflict and so provide no respite from the original burden of stress. They are "nonbehaviors" and are toxic; they leave you saddled with the original conflict.

With the other four choices, the danger is in limiting yourself to a single response, since each response is appropriate in different contexts. That is, there are times to quit the job; and there are other times to try and get the job function changed; and there are other times to acquire new ways of working and reacting on the job; and there are other times when the most appropriate response is to alter your perception of what's happening so that your feelings naturally and automatically change.

Enlarging your range of responses in this way serves two purposes: it protects you from being caught helplessly in conflicts with limited power to act, and it reveals to you when the only reasonable alternative available is to quit.

STRATEGIES TO GET PAY INCREASES

Raises are most frequently gained by those who have sized up the situation and handled it with finesse rather than guile. Start preparing for your salary increase when you start a job. Find out how the company identifies an outstanding performer.

Successful raise seekers usually combine a high degree of determination with an unabrasive personality. They are not easily put off, and at the same time, they do not put others off. They avoid the blunder of putting the boss in a defensive position that provokes a counterattack. They avoid conversations regarding salary increases that center on why it's necessary rather than on why the company should want to award it.

Make a list of your accomplishments. Be prepared to state them with assurance and pride. Remember to concentrate your energies on presenting the parts of your job that are judged to have corporate value. Work visibly; don't hide your light under a bushel. If you do more than is expected of you, be sure the boss knows it.

Another point to consider is keeping at least one foot in the marketplace, no matter how pleased you are with your current position. Knowing that others are interested in your talents is a powerful source of confidence and improves your negotiating power.

KEEPING YOURSELF UPDATED

It is your responsibility to make preparations for your next job while you're still on this one. That doesn't mean diverting your energy from doing your best on your present assignment but rather maintaining ongoing awareness of your own career objectives, your skill development and work accomplishments, and those people and organizations that might enable you to realize your goals. To this end, develop and keep up-to-date information files for future use, either within your present organization or in introducing you to a new company.

Skills and Accomplishments

In your work to design a strong resume, you developed a list of your personal accomplishments and grouped them under the headings of specific professional skills. This will be the beginning of an ongoing file of your work and achievements. Add to the list weekly as you explore the week's work to identify those accomplishments that you were wholly or partially responsible for. Using the list of action verbs in the first section of this manual, itemize your achievements during the week: I organized . . . ; I designed . . . ; I developed . . . ; I revised . . . ; I wrote . . . ; etc. Try to add to each what the impact of the achievement was in your organization or agency. Did it lead to increased efficiency? Additional profits? Better staff relationships? Additional cooperation? The acceptance of a contract or proposal? The attainment of an organizational goal? Fewer product returns? More sales? Greater savings?

Keep this list going. Every month or two, organize the accomplishments into groupings that communicate some of your basic functional skills: management, communications, selling, supervision, coordination, planning, conflict management, motivation, administration, production, problem solving, negotiating, evaluating, etc.

Contacts

In your efforts to locate your present job, you developed a list of potentially helpful contacts, both personal and professional. Your new work brings you into contact with new people, some of whom get to know and respect you and your work. Maintain a list of these people—their addresses, their professional roles, what your contact was, when you were in touch, your sense of their availability to you. Should the day arrive that you are ready to leave your present job and move to another company or even another area of endeavor, these are the people who know your skills, talents, style, energy, and accomplishments. These are the people who may well be pleased to be able to serve you in your new search.

Keep up the contacts with your business friends and professional associates. Few people enjoy being called upon only when there is a need that they can fill.

Potential Target Companies

This list will include all the companies you originally contacted in your job search that you never followed through on because you accepted your present position. It will also include all the companies your present job puts you in contact with that you find yourself admiring in terms of staff, organizational objectives, personnel policies, professional reputation, etc. For each company, a potential target should the time arise, make note of the names of those individuals who head the departments that interest you, the individuals that your contact with the company has evidenced are the decision makers.

REASSESSMENT

As a result of what you've learned from your feedback network and your self-evaluative work, you are ready to assess yourself anew in your present job. This determination will influence your career focus in the future.

Which of the following conclusions come closest to where you are?

1. I am currently in a good situation and want to do everything I can to maintain my present level of satisfaction and achievement.
2. I am currently in a fine situation, but there are a few rough spots that need some smoothing.
3. I am going to stay in my present job, but I'm going to begin to look for new challenges that will expand it.
4. I like what I'm doing, but this department or this organization is not for me, and I'm going to look for another environment in which to do this work.
5. I like the organization I'm with, the structure and the ambiance, but the particular work I'm doing is not rewarding and I'm going to look around within the organization to find another niche for myself.
6. I'm in the wrong job for me; it's time to look elsewhere and find something new.
7. I plan to make a career change, but this isn't the appropriate time to do so. I can make plans now, but it would be unwise to act.

8. I plan to make a career change that will take some preparation; I can begin now to ready myself by enrolling in suitable courses and training workshops.

9. I want to continue basically in my present career, but I want to be self-employed. I'll begin now to research the opportunities and obstacles to my proceeding as a consultant or starting my own business.

SUMMING UP

In the course of working through this manual, you strove to find the answers to three basic questions:

1. Where am I now?
2. Where do I want to be?
3. How can I get from here to there?

You wrote, and thought, and listed, and designed, and communicated, and responded, and planned, and implemented, and organized, and sold, and coordinated, and evaluated, and developed, and achieved.

You have exhibited these skills and gained the use of many tools. You know how to use self-evaluative inventories, work experience and skill-based resumes, broadcast letters, time management action plans, contact networks, search firms, support and communications networks, and feedback.

Many of these tools are multipurposed. They will continue to serve you even now that you've found your job. The inventories will help you to continually reassess your present comfort and performance at work. The time management action plan is a model for thinking through and implementing work objectives. Developing networks enables you to be thoroughly aware and powerful in your organization. These and some of the other tools and exercises in this manual are adaptable for your ongoing use. Still others you will put aside and refer to when you decide to make further advances in your career.

You've come to the end of this manual. And, as in so many other areas, to make an ending is to make a beginning. What you begin now is the delightful task of monitoring your own personal and career objectives, of resting when it's time to rest and moving when it's time to move. The reward before you is a productive and satisfying work life.

Appendixes

APPENDIX I
DEFINING MANAGEMENT FUNCTIONS

All managers concern themselves with two general types of work—management and operational. The ratio between the two will vary from one manager to another, depending upon the individual, the management level, the type of effort supervised, and the management environment.

It is generally recognized by writers in the field of management that management work is comprised of five basic functions: planning, organizing, staffing, directing, and controlling. These functions are further broken down into supporting activities.

Planning: Determining what work must be done. Activities include:

1. Defining roles and missions. Determining the nature and scope of the work to be performed.
2. Forecasting. Determining where you should invest your time, energy, and talent.
3. Identifying indicators of effectiveness. Determining measurable factors on which you can gauge your success, and the success of others, in meeting goals.
4. Selecting and setting objectives. Determining results to be achieved.
5. Preparing action plans. Determining how to achieve your specific objectives.
   (a) Programming. Establishing a sequence of actions to follow in reaching objectives.
   (b) Reviewing and reconciling. Testing and revising a tentative plan, as needed, prior to commitment to action.
   (c) Budgeting. Determining and assigning the necessary resources required to reach your goals.
   (d) Fixing accountability. Determining who will take the responsibility for the accomplishment of the work to be performed.
   (e) Policymaking. Establishing rules, regulations, etc.
   (f) Establishing procedures. Determining consistent and systematic methods of handling work.

In studying these activities, can you see where you have achieved and contributed to your management career advancement? If so, remember to use these definitions in stating your job accomplishments.

Organizing: Classifying and dividing the work you do and are responsible for into manageable units. Activities include:

1. Structuring. Grouping the work you do and supervise into effective and efficient production.

2. Integrating. Establishing conditions to allow your subordinates and peers to work in an effective climate that creates teamwork. All managers and supervisors perform the function of organizing work. The difference is only a matter of degree.

Staffing: Determining the requirements for and ensuring the availability of personnel to perform the work. Activities include:

1. Determining personnel needs. Analyzing the work to decide what personnel is necessary to carry out the work.
2. Selecting personnel. Identifying potential employees and appointing them to organizational positions.
3. Developing personnel. Providing opportunities for your people to increase their capabilities in line with organizational needs.

Directing: Bringing about the human activity required to accomplish objectives. Activities include:

1. Assigning. Charging individual employees with job responsibilities or tasks to be performed.
2. Motivating. Influencing people to perform in a desired manner.
3. Communicating. Achieving effective flow of ideas and information in desired directions.
4. Coordinating. Achieving harmony of group effort toward accomplishment of individual or group goals.

As you review the functions and activities of directing, you will see that this is the area where first-line and middle managers spend the largest percentage of time. Be sure you identify your key accomplishments in this area.

Controlling: Assuring the effective accomplishment of goals. Activities include:

1. Establishing standards. Devising a gauge of successful performance in achieving goals.
2. Measuring performance. Assessing actual versus planned performance.
3. Taking corrective action. Bringing about performance improvements to meet goals.

Go back and review all the important jobs you have held. Define the job and identify the key management functions you performed. Or look at your past experience as functions that may be management oriented. Review the various activities you undertook to support each function.

You are going to identify yourself as a results-oriented person. The accomplishments that you use in your personal marketing efforts should reflect the results you have achieved in these management activities. From studying the preceding functions and activities, identify your work achievements and precisely project your management image.

Following are examples of accomplishments that support management activities:

- Classified and divided work activities in the accounting department. Resulted in labor savings of $20,000 per month.
- Determined systematic methods of handling labor grievances. Reduced second-step hearings by 50 percent without increasing man-hours.
- Established conditions for effective teamwork; increased productivity by 30 percent by allowing personnel to define personal work goals.
- Reduced the time needed in operations by 35 percent.

You could now perform a similar exercise, identifying particular activities that are operational in nature. For example, what accomplishments have you attained in the following areas: customer contact, administration, staff duties, report writing, verbal presentations, and personnel?

APPENDIX 2
REFERENCE TOOLS

The following are available at your local public library or may be ordered from the addresses given.

American Electronics Association Directory. American Electronics Association, 2600 El Camino Road, Palo Alto, California 94306.

Lists alphabetically over a thousand member electronic companies, naming top officers and marketed manufactured products. Included is a supplement of all electronic companies in the United States. Published annually.

Business Directory, Chamber of Commerce.

The directory includes major employers, Chamber member businesses and their presidents or managers, Buyers Guide (merchandise and services), Standard Industrial Classification, businesses listed by communities, trade and professional organizations. It is available in each city through the local Chamber of Commerce.

Business Periodicals Index

A subject index to selected periodicals in the field of accounting, advertising, public relations, automation, banking, communications, economics, finance and investments, insurance, labor management, marketing, taxation, and specific business, industries, and trades. Classified chronologically.

Career Opportunity Index for the West, Professional Edition.
Career Research Systems, Inc., 1979.

This edition provides employment opportunities projected by employers. Addressed primarily to employment in California, it includes most western states and a special section on southern California.

Catalyst Career Options Series.
Catalyst National Headquarters, 14 E. 60th St., New York, New York 10022.

Prepared for women but also useful for men, a set of pamphlets to bring goals into focus and launch an effective job campaign in the following fields: accounting, advertising, banking, business administration, communications, counseling, data processing, education, engineering, environmental affairs, finance, fund raising, health services, industrial management, insurance planning for work, publishing, real estate, recreation, retailing, sales, teaching. Order directly from Catalyst National Headquarters.

Contacts Influential.
Influential Contacts Ltd., Inc., Weatherly Building, 15 SE Morrison, Portland, Oregon 97214.

A complete catalog of all firms and key personnel, arranged alphabetically by kind of business, zip code areas, personal names of key executives and numerically by telelphone number and Standard Industrial Classification (SIC).

Dictionary of Occupational Titles.
U.S. Department of Labor. 4th Edition. Washington, D.C.: Government Printing Office.

This dictionary, often called the DOT, provides code numbers and standardized comprehensive descriptions of 20,000 job titles, covering nearly all jobs in the U.S. economy.

It groups job titles together according to interrelationship of job duties and requirements. It also includes an alphabetical index and a grouping by industry.

Directory of Corporate Affiliations 1979.
National Register Publishing Co., Inc., 5201 Old Orchard Road, Skokie, Illinois 60077.

Designed to give an in-depth view of United States corporations. Literally a "Who Owns Whom" listed by parent companies and their divisions, subsidiaries, and affiliates plus a cross-reference index to subsidiaries and divisions. Published annually.

Dun and Bradstreet Reference Book of Corporate Managements.
Dun and Bradstreet, Inc., 99 Church St., New York, New York 10007.

This volume contains data on directors and selected officers of approximately 2,400 companies. These are companies with annual sales of $20 million or more and/or 1,000 or more employees. The data on these individuals include date of birth, education, and business positions presently and previously held. Published annually.

Encyclopedia of Associations.
Gale Research Company, Book Tower, Detroit, Michigan 48226.

Three volumes—Volumes 1 and 2 contain a comprehensive list of all types of national associations, arranged by broad classification, with an alphabetical keyword index. Gives names of chief officers, brief statement of activities, numbers of members, and names of publications. Volume 3 contains a quarterly list of "New Associations and Projects." Published annually.

Encyclopedia of Business Information Sources.
Paul Wasserman, Gale Research Company, Book Tower, Detroit, Michigan 48226.

Arranged in dictionary form, this book lists publications and sources of information on such categories as the line of business, specific products and processes, and particular functions and services. Covers fields of business from artificial limbs to financial advertising to the underwear industry. Published annually.

Encyclopedia of Careers and Vocational Guidance.
Two volumes. Garden City, N.Y.: Doubleday.

Volume 1, "Planning Your Career," describes career opportunities in major industries.

Volume 2, "Careers and Occupations," describes specific occupations, with information on education and training, conditions of work, employment outlook, chances for advancement, social and psychological factors, and earnings.

Encyclopedia of Geographic Information Sources.
Paul Wasserman, Gale Research Company, Book Tower, Detroit, Michigan 48226.

A geographic source book that provides a minibibliography of sources on particular aspects of cities, states, and countries around the world. Covers geographic areas, from marketing in the Dominican Republic to directories in Singapore to the Chamber of Commerce in the United Arab Republic. Sources in the United States are listed by states and major cities.

Funk and Scott Index of Corporations and Industries.

An index to articles on companies and industries that have appeared in selected financial publications and brokerage reports.

Geographical Index to the Directory of Corporate Affiliations 1979.
National Register Publishing Co., Inc., 5201 Old Orchard Road, Skokie, Illinois 60077.

Accompanies the *Directory of Corporate Affiliations,* with corporations listed geographically.

Million Dollar Directory, 2 Vols.
Dun and Bradstreet, Inc., 99 Church Street, New York, New York 10007.

Volume 1 lists 31,000 United States companies with an indicated net worth of $1 million or more. Gives officers, products, SIC codes, sales, and numbers of employees. The yellow pages list companies geographically and the blue pages list companies by SIC. At the end of this directory is an alphabetical list of executives and directors.

Volume 2, "The Middle Market," contains identical information for companies with a net worth of $500,000–$999,000.

Moody's Industrial Manual, Volumes 1 and 2.
Moody's Investors Services, Inc., New York, 1979.

Contains a brief history of company and its operations, subsidiaries, plants; products; officers and directors; comparative income statements; balance sheets; description of outstanding securities. Center blue pages provide useful data, including price ranges of outstanding stock. Classification of this information is by industry and product. Also includes information on mergers and acquisitions.

National Trade and Professional Associations of the United States and Canada Labor Unions.
Columbia Books, Inc., Washington, D.C.

Alphabetical list of over 4,300 national trade and professional associations, with key word and executive indexes. Gives chief officers, number of members, annual budgets, and publications.

Occupational Outlook Handbook.
U.S. Bureau of Labor Statistics.

Revised every two years. Washington, D.C.: Government Printing Office.

Describes several hundred occupations, including information on required training, employment outlook, earnings, and working conditions. The descriptions are grouped into 13 clusters of related jobs.

Introductory chapters describe important occupational and industrial trends. Another section discusses the outlook for over 30 industries.

Small Business Bibliographies.
Small Business Administration, Washington, D.C.

Pamphlets listing trade journals and government and nongovernment publications in such fields as advertising, buying, data processing, inventory management, library reference, manufacturing, management, motels, personnel management, retailing, tourism, and wholesaling.

Standard and Poor's Register of Corporations, Directors and Executives 1979, Corporations, Volume 1.
Standard and Poor's Corporation, 25 Broadway, New York, New York 10004.

Alphabetical listing by business name of approximately 37,000 corporations, including zip codes; telephone numbers; names, title, and other functions of approximately 390,000 officers, directors, and other principals; SIC codes; annual sales and number of employees; divisions and subsidiaries; principal business affiliations; and addresses of executives.

Standard and Poor's Register of Corporations, Directors and Executives 1979, Volume 2.
Standard and Poor's Corporation, 25 Broadway, New York, New York 10004.
Straight alphabetical list of 75,000 individuals serving as officers, directors, trustees, partners, etc. of United States corporations. Provides principal business affiliation, addresses, college attended, fraternity membership, and year and place of birth.

Standard and Poor's Register of Corporations, Directors and Executives 1979, Indexes.
Standard and Poor's Corporation, 25 Broadway, New York, New York 10004.
Divided into color-coded sections: Standard Industrial Classification, obituary (deaths within past year), new individual names appearing for the first time in the register, and new companies appearing for the first time in the register.

Standard Directory of Advertisers 1979.
National Register Publishing Co., Inc., 5201 Old Orchard Road, Skokie, Illinois 60077.
List of over 17,000 advertiser companies allotting annual appropriations for national or regional advertising campaigns. Indexed alphabetically by trade name and by classification (heating, watercraft, travel, etc.)

Standard Industrial Classification Manual 1972.
United States Office of Management and Budget, U.S. Government Printing Office, Washington, D.C.
The SIC numerically classifies all establishments by the type of activity in which they are engaged. It is intended to cover the entire field of economic activities from agriculture to manufacturing to repair services. Includes a 1977 supplement.

Thomas Register of American Manufacturers. 11 Vols.
Thomas Publishing Company, New York, 1979.
Volumes 1–6 list manufacturers by specific product. Volume 7 is an alphabetical list of companies, giving address, branch offices, subsidiaries, products, estimated capitalization, and occasionally principal officers. Volume 8 is an index to product classifications and includes a list of leading trade names (contained in pink sheets), boards of trade, chambers of commerce. Volumes 9–11 are catalogs of companies.

Walker's Manual of Western Corporations 1979. Volumes 1 and 2.
Walker's Manual Incorporated, 3855 Naples Plaza, Long Beach, California 90803.

Describes and lists alphabetically financial institutions and corporations publicly owned and headquartered in the 13 western states and western Canada. Also includes a geographic and industry classification index.

Manufacturer's Register.
Times Mirror Company, Times Mirror Square, Los Angeles, California 90053.

Manufacturers are listed three ways: alphabetical section, which contains all available information; geographical section, which lists plants by name and product; and products and services section.

INDEX

accomplishment(s), job
  categories for defining, 153–155
  detailing, during interviews, 119
  exploring (exercises), 35–37, 42–43
  importance of, to prospective employ-
    ers, 37–38
  interviews and, 116, 125
  records, importance of maintaining,
    147
  statements, *see* accomplishment state-
    ments, job
  using, for pay increases, 146
accomplishment statements, job
  action verbs for preparing (examples),
    40
  elements of, 38–39
  examples of, 41–42
acknowledgement letter
  example of, 133
  use of, 132
action plan(s)
  assignment of priorities within, 111
  developing, 108
  implementation of, as key to successful
    job searching, 111
  importance of, in job search campaign,
    108
  management of time and, 108–109
  organization of, 111
  reviewing, for negotiations, 134
  time management (example), 109
action verbs (examples), 40
advancement, career, *see* mobility, upward
advertisements, newspaper, *see* classified
  want ads
acquisitions, job, Department of Labor
  statistics on, 63
advertising of skills
  through classified want ads, 96
  through contact network, 63–66
  contacts and, 64
  through employment agencies,
    101–102
  through executive search firms,
    102–107
  follow-up, 66–70

through job applications, 93–94
job search strategy for, 71–80
mass, 82–93
personal resources and, 63
print media as aid in, 96–100
references as additional method of,
  107–108
see also marketing strategy, self-
agencies, employment, *see* employment
  agencies
*American Electronics Association Di-
  rectory,* as reference tool, 155
attitude, positive, and career success, 2,
  118, 123–124
"analysis and prediction"
  defined, 35
  use of, 36–37
applicant testing, by executive search
  firms, 128
applications, job
  completing, 94
  job interviews and, 93–94
  personal data sheet for, 95
  as screening devices, 93
associations, professional, as means of
  contacting target companies, 75

behavior, as type of feedback, 140
benefits, company, description of, 130
broadcast letters
  defined, 82
  examples of, 85–91
  follow-up of, 93
  introductory statements for, 83–84
  recording data from, importance of, 93
  third party, 84, 92
  tips in preparing, 83
  see also tailor-made letters
Bureau of Labor Statistics, on career
  changes, 2
*Business Directory, Chamber of Com-
  merce,* as reference tool, 155
business contacts, 64, 72
business news, personal, 101
business objectives, *see* objectives, business